AMOS

A STUDY GUIDE
COMMENTARY

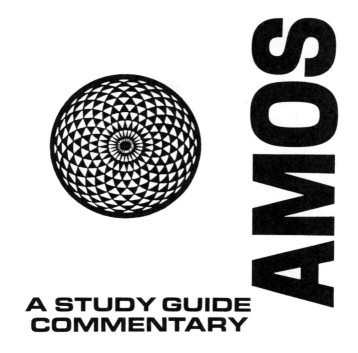

AMOS

A STUDY GUIDE
COMMENTARY

D. DAVID GARLAND

ZONDERVAN
PUBLISHING HOUSE

OF THE ZONDERVAN CORPORATION
GRAND RAPIDS, MICHIGAN 49506

AMOS

Copyright 1966 by
Zondervan Publishing House
Grand Rapids, Michigan

Seventh printing   1978
ISBN 0-310-24833-7

Printed in the United States of America

Dedicated to
ELLENOR, JANE ELLEN
AND DAVID MARSHALL

PREFACE

This book represents an attempt to provide the layman with a brief volume using the thematic approach to the book of Amos. It is not a critical study. It was written with the hope that the reader would use it alongside his open Bible.

To serve its purpose best the student should first read the Scripture references in the section headings and then read the materials written here which attempt to explain the basic meaning of the portion already read.

This volume does not endeavor to be exhaustive. It is an attempt to deal with the great themes of the book and the prophet's method of handling them.

I am indebted to Zondervan for requesting the manuscript, my teachers for an interest in the prophets, my colleagues and Mrs. H. C. Brown, who read the manuscript, the Administration of Southwestern Baptist Theological Seminary for allowing me the time to write, and Mrs. Delbert Taylor for typing the manuscript.

D. DAVID GARLAND

Southwestern Baptist Theological Seminary
Fort Worth, Texas

CONTENTS

A STUDY GUIDE
COMMENTARY

AMOS

CHAPTER 1

INTRODUCING THE PROPHET

The first of the writing prophets — so designated because their words were recorded in books bearing their names — was Amos. According to the general title (1:1), Amos was a shepherd from Tekoa who prophesied to Israel during the reigns of Uzziah in Judah and Jeroboam II in Israel — two years before the earthquake.

1. *The Personal History of Amos.* Tekoa may or may not have been the birthplace of Amos, but it was now his home. The village was located about six miles from Bethlehem and twelve miles from Jerusalem, some 3,000 feet above sea level. From this point one can see the mountains of Moab in the distance and the Dead Sea below. This region was located in a rugged area which came to be known as the "wilderness of Judea." It was the same general area that John the Baptist roamed and in which Jesus was tempted.

The family of Amos is not mentioned in the book containing his prophecies. This omission has been generally taken to mean that he came from a humble home and parentage. If this assumption is correct, then his family lacked social and economic status. He belonged to the poorer class of Judah and doubtless felt the same afflictions in his own country that he later condemned during his ministry to the north.

2. *The Date of the Prophet.* In the opening verse of the book we learn that Amos' ministry was during the reigns of Uzziah (783-742 b.c.) in Judah and Jeroboam II (786-746 b.c.) in Israel. This would mean that he prophesied, or at least began to prophesy, between 786 and 742 b.c. It is generally suggested, however, that his active ministry should be dated somewhere around 765-750 b.c. This period has been preferred because it would have allowed sufficient time for the expansion and the prosperity associated with the reigns of Kings Jeroboam II and Uzziah. It would also indicate that his ministry was concluded before the period of anarchy following Jeroboam II (II Kings 15:8-28) since such conditions are not alluded to in any of the messages of the prophet.

Some have attempted to date the prophet upon the basis of the references to the earthquake in 1:1; 5:8, and 8:9 and in Zechariah 14:5ff. The earthquake possibly occurred in association with a total eclipse of the sun on June 15, 763 b.c. If such should be fact, and there is no way of absolute determination, then Amos would date from 765 b.c. Whichever method is used to approach the dating, and the former seems preferable, it would seem that the dates 765-750 b.c. would be as accurate as any.

3. *The Occupation of Amos.* The chief occupation of the prophet was that of herdsman. He was the keeper of *nakad* — a small, short-limbed sheep, noted for its choice wool. Along with his shepherding, he had as a secondary occupation the tending of a grove of sycamore trees which likely stood on the slopes leading down to the Dead Sea. The sycamore produced a fig-like fruit, which supplemented the diet of the poor and probably provided them additional income.

The exact nature of the task of "a pincher of sycamore trees" (7:14) is uncertain. The duties may have simply included pruning and tending the trees in general. It has been theorized, however, that the task involved provoking the fruit to ripen by bruising it in the hands or between the fingers. It has also been suggested that the care of the trees involved the breaking of the skin of the fruit either to allow the bitter juices to drain from it or to allow an otherwise harmful insect to escape. It is, of course, possible that all of these duties were involved in the occupation.

In addition to being a keeper of sheep and a pincher of sycamores, Amos was doubtless responsible for the disposition of his wool and sycamore fruit. He would take his products to the trade centers of the Northern Kingdom, where he could, in all likelihood, get a better price than in Judah. Such trips afforded him the opportunity to learn of the conditions existing in the country to the north and gave him the knowledge which would equip him for the ministry awaiting him.

4. *The Times of Amos.* National independence and prosperity characterized the times of Amos. During the time of Jehu (842-815 B.C.) and Jehoahaz (815-801 B.C.), Israel had been sorely threatened by the Syrians (II Kings 10:32, 33; 13:3, 7). When Joash (801-786 B.C.) came to the throne, conditions changed (II Kings 13:25). The change was unquestionably brought about by the Assyrian threat to Syria, a threat which ultimately resulted in her overthrow by the Assyrians, who destroyed the capital during the reign of Adad-nirari III (811-783 B.C.). As a result of this overthrow, Israel was relieved of one of her greatest oppressors.

After their victory over the Syrians, the Assyrians entered a period of decline which removed them as a threat to Israel also. At this same time, Egypt was weakened by internal dissension and disorganization. All of these conditions developing at one time enabled Israel to get on her feet. She began by expanding her trade and her economy in general. This expansion was greatly accelerated by the fact that her resources were no longer required as tribute to one of her previous oppressors. Therefore, Israel, along with Judah, entered an era of freedom and prosperity unrivaled by any other in their history.

The advantages now realized were not enjoyed by all the people of the nation, however. The middle class had disappeared. Their departure left but two classes, the rich and the poor. As is so often the case, the rich grew richer and the poor poorer. Injustice became widespread as the rich gained economic ad-

vantages which were all too often secured through the unjusti-
fiable friendliness and favoritism of their leaders and courts.

In addition to increased economic development and independence, the period was marked by great religious activity.
During this time the inhabitants doubtless increased the number of their worship centers and multiplied their offerings and
sacrifices (4:4, 5) beyond all legal requirements. Even so, their
religious fervor failed to affect the quality of their day-to-day
living. This failure resulted in injustice, inhumanity, and unconcern for the needs of others as well as a moral decadence
unparalleled in Israel's history (2:6-8). Such conditions as these
called for a strong and courageous voice. That voice was to be
the voice of Amos.

5. *Amos the Man.* Conditions in Israel demanded a man of
extraordinary commitment, courage, simplicity and faith. Amos
possessed these qualities and charactertics in a remarkable way.

First, he was a man with a *sense of call* (7:14, 15). He early
disassociated himself from the prophetic guild. This was a guild
of professional prophets who were motivated primarily by what
they could personally gain through their work. In announcing
that "I was no prophet, neither the son of a prophet" (7:14), he
was denying any relationship to them. In the first phrase, "I
was no prophet," he denied being a prophet in the ordinary and
popular sense. He denied being one of those who for a price
spoke what men wanted to hear.

The second phrase, "neither the son of a prophet," may
carry through the idea that he did not belong to the group, or it
may have meant that his father was not a prophet, and therefore
he had not inherited his office. In either case, he was seeking
to identify himself with the true prophets. This group consisted of those laid hold upon by the Spirit of God and commanded to "go, prophesy unto my people Israel" (7:15). These
were prophets, not by birth or chosen profession, but by right
of God's having taken them and having commissioned them.
To this group Amos belonged.

Second, he was a *man with a message from God.* As a result of his having been commissioned, Amos said, "Now there-

fore hear thou the word of the Lord: Thou sayest, prophesy not against Israel, and drop not thy word against the house of Isaac. Therefore thus saith the Lord . . ." (7:16, 17a). In so speaking, Amos declared that the source of his message was God. He claimed to be speaking for God — a claim which he consistently made in using the words, "thus saith the Lord." Though the words which he spoke came from his lips, their ultimate source was the God of Israel. He spoke for God as he received his message from God.

Third, he was a *courageous man*. Perhaps Amos' greatest display of courage was in his denouncing the king as well as the religious leaders for their part in allowing and encouraging the conditions which existed in Israel (7:10, 11, 16, 17). It took no small courage to condemn the king under any condition. To condemn him at the royal sanctuary was an unheard of thing; yet Amos did not hesitate to do so (7:12, 13). Even in the face of threat and implied intimidation (7:12), he persisted in declaring the word which he had received. Though it may have endangered his life, there was no hesitancy nor compromise on his part. He was committed to declare the word of God wherever, whenever, and to whomever God directed. He knew no fear; he gave no ground in performing the will of God or in proclaiming his truth.

Fourth, there was a *simplicity about his message*. Few indeed, if any at all, had to ask the prophet or any other person what Amos meant by what he said. His words were simple and pointed. Men understood what he said as well as what he meant, and they reacted rather quickly (7:12, 13). Even today there is relatively little difficulty in understanding what the prophet was saying or what it means for every generation.

Fifth, he was a *man of remarkable faith*. In face of the sin within the nation and the impending judgment of God upon the chosen people, Amos did not despair of the purpose of God. He saw the future as a time when God would build as "in the days of old" (9:11). The nation would, in time to come — after the announced judgment — be restored, conquer her enemies, and realize an unprecedented prosperity which would not fail (9:

11-15). He believed in the ultimate realization of that which God had purposed at the time He chose Israel. The future will see the plan, the purpose and dream of God realized, not in the nation itself but in the remnant. God would raise up the "tabernacle of David" in the Messianic Kingdom of the future. That which God had begun He would accomplish. If it could not be realized in Israel, it would be in the remnant. There was a future!

6. *The General Title of the Book of Amos.* Amos 1:1 is the title of the book. It sets forth a statement concerning Amos, his occupation, and the time in which he lived, as well as the content of the book. The book consists of "the words . . . which he saw concerning Israel in the days of Uzziah king of Judah, and in the days of Jeroboam, the son of Joash king of Israel, two years before the earthquake."

7. *The Summary of the Message of Amos* (1:2). The summary of the message of Amos is given in a poetic statement that sets forth the nature and extent of the judgment which was to fall upon the nation. It was to be a judgment which not only affected mankind, but also the natural order. In declaring that Yahweh "will roar from Zion" (His earthly habitation) in judgment, the prophet was drawing an analogy in which he compared the judgment of God with the roar of the lion. Amos had doubtless heard the roar of the lions as he lay out under the stars at night. To hear such a roar conveyed to every hearer the fact that the lion was about to leap upon its prey. The roar of Yahweh from Zion indicated — declared — that He was about to fall upon Israel as the lion fell upon its prey. Israel would be as helpless as a lamb in the clutches of a lion when Yahweh brought judgment upon the nation. The judgment which was about to befall Israel would express itself in desolation — a desolation so great that the dried-up pastures are said to mourn. The devastation would reach all the way to Carmel, the most fertile area, the last and least to suffer from drought and desolation. In so depicting the devastation, the prophet was simply saying that there would be no area, however protected or secure, which would not suffer as a result of the judgment announced

by the roar from Zion (1:2). God was on His way to pour forth His wrath. There would not be one of the guilty nor any place of their dwelling to escape its reach and consequence.

The remainder of the book of Amos is given over to an amplification of these summary words.

FOR FURTHER STUDY

1. For a discussion of the conditions in Israel at the time of Amos read pp. 234-248 in *A History of Israel* by John Bright.
2. Read the article on "Tekoa" in *The Interpreter's Dictionary of the Bible*, Volume IV, pp. 527-529 or *The Zondervan Pictorial Bible Dictionary*, p. 829; also see "Amos" on pp. 36 and 37 of *The Zondervan Pictorial Bible Dictionary*.
   (From this point on *The Interpreter's Dictionary of the Bible* will be referred to as IDB and *The Zondervan Pictorial Bible Dictionary* as ZPBD.)
3. Read the article on "Jerusalem" in ZPBD and IDB, Volume II, pp. 843-866 and the one on "Carmel" in Volume I, p. 538.
4. List some of the favorable as well as unfavorable conditions in Israel which have parallels in modern society.
5. What should the modern prophet do in light of any unfavorable parallels?

CHAPTER 2

WEAVING THE WEB
(Amos 1:3 - 2:16)

The primary task of Amos was the arraignment of Israel. He condemned every form of injustice and inhumanity practiced in the Northern Kingdom. On first thought one might expect that a prophet to Israel would tend to ignore the other nations existing at the time of his ministry, yet quite the contrary was true in the case of Amos. He condemned the surrounding nations as forthrightly as he did his own nation (Judah) and Israel to whom he was sent to prophesy.

The prophet's condemnation of the nations must have been based upon his concept of God and His creation. He doubtless saw himself and all other men as having been created by God. He and they had been created in the image of God. Since the Creator was a moral being, those created in His image were also. Therefore, every moral standard set by the Creator was to be observed by every man whether a citizen of a covenant nation or not. Any man or any nation ignoring God's standard or refusing to meet it was placed under judgment.

21

Since the nations surrounding Israel had been as guilty of not meeting the standard as Israel and Judah, both covenant nations, they were as deserving of the prophet's words of condemnation and of divine judgment as those having a special relationship to God. Therefore, Amos wasted little time in calling them to task. In fact, this was where he began.

Before turning to deal with the prophet's words to the nations, one must remember to keep in mind that practically all these nations had been long-standing enemies of Israel. The conflicts growing out of their enmity had inevitably left deep scars upon Israel. The condemnation of these who had been their enemies would have been welcomed by many of Israel's citizens. They had in all likelihood been waiting for someone to appear who would call their enemies to task. Amos under divine direction would capitalize on their anticipation.

If the prophecies spoken against Israel's neighbors were spoken in the order in which they occur in the book of Amos, then he used the attitude of Israel toward the nations to a great psychological advantage. For all the while he was condemning the nations, he would be gaining the favor of Israel. This may have been a vital part of his strategy as he planned to deal with Israel. In condemning sin after sin among the nations, he was building a strong case against every form of sin. He was seeking to establish the fact that sin among any nation and every nation would provoke God to judgment. With his case made, Amos would turn to denounce the sins of the covenant nations, of Judah and Israel.

It was as though the prophet were weaving a web. He, first, circumscribed Israel by moving from one nation to another describing their sins and condemning them on their account. It was a web in which he would eventually ensnare Israel and establish for all to see the guilt of those commissioned "to be a blessing." In doing so he suggested that their guilt would, if anything, be greater than that of the nations because of the covenant which existed between Israel and God. He was raising the question, "If the sin of the nations could not be ignored, how could Israel expect to go unpunished?" Watch as Amos weaves his web.

1. *Judgment upon Damascus* (1:3-5). From the time of Solomon (1 Kings 11:23-25) there had been tension and conflict between Syria and Israel (compare II Kings 10:32ff.; 13:3, 5, 7, 22). It was an enmity which had grown with the years (I Kings 15:16ff.). To have a prophet pronounce judgment upon this long-standing enemy to the north and east would be a source of great delight to many in Israel.

To strengthen his case, Amos began by emphasizing the fact that the message which he spoke was from God — he was a spokesman (1:3a). The message was not one of personal hostility and hatred — it was from God. Having established the source of his message, he began by pronouncing judgment upon Damascus, the capital of Syria (reputed by some to be the oldest city in the world). He evidently used Damascus to represent the entire nation; it stood for all of Syria. The condemnation involved "three transgressions of Damascus, yea, . . . four." The number three as used here infers completeness, fullness or the whole measure. He was saying that the sin of Syria was full. It was more than full — it was overflowing. The words "yea, for four" added to "three transgressions" suggests that the ultimate — the climax or the breaking point — in sin had been reached. Their sin was more than could be tolerated any longer. Nothing but judgment could result from sin of this degree and force.

The sin condemned was "transgressions." The Hebrew word used is rebellion and means that their sin was rebelling against God. This would indicate that Amos believed that the nations outside the covenant were as responsible for the standards of righteousness established by Yahweh and must suffer the consequences of not measuring up the same as those within the covenant.

Rebellion was a word often used by the prophet to characterize sin. It denotes an ugly spirit and a haughty attitude. Such sin could not go unpunished — judgment would inevitably come upon those guilty of it. Because of the sins of Damascus (Syria) God would not turn back the deserved punishment. The punishment was announced as the intolerable point of sin was reached when Syria threshed Gilead (II Kings 10:32, 33) with instruments of iron — a custom believed by some to have been used by oriental nations upon their prisoners at this time. It involved the dragging of threshing instruments similar to a modern section-harrow across the bodies of their captives and thereby mutilating them. Whether this was an actual practice or just a description of their evil practices, we may never know. Yet whatever the case, such practices suggest disdain for man and excessive cruelty on the part of Syria. Such inhumanity could not go unpunished.

In return for their wickedness God would send a "fire" (a term used to depict the devastation of war) upon the house (land) of Hazael, founder of the ruling dynasty in Syria during Amos' time. The onslaught would topple the palaces of the ruling monarch, Ben-hadad III, after destroying the bar of the defenses of Damascus (1:5), the bar being a metal piece used to bar the city gate and used here to symbolize all her defenses. There would be no escape to the pleasant and secure abodes of the past — the Valley of Aven, a fertile region in Syria associated, as some suggest, with abundance, and the House of Eden or Beth-eden, probably the luxurious seat of one of the officials in Syria. All the inhabitants, rulers as well as citizens, would be exiled to Kir, the ancient home of their forefathers (9:7).

Upon the completion of this pronouncement of judgment there must have been a sense of rejoicing on the part of those who heard the prophet. An ancient enemy was coming under judgment. The nation would be glad. They must have felt that their neighbor to the north and east deserved all that the prophet predicted, and they could hardly wait to see it come to pass.

Though Amos did not state precisely how the judgment was to be accomplished, it is believed by many to have been realized in the assault of the Assyrians, who marched against Syria in response to the request of Ahaz (II Kings 16:5ff.). The Assyrians overthrew them, destroyed their king, and led many into captivity.

2. *Judgment upon Philistia* (1:6-8). Having dealt with Israel's neighbor to the north and east, Amos then turned to Philistia on the south and west. Like Syria, the Philistines had been a long-standing enemy of Israel (Judges 14ff.; I Samuel 4; 13; 31; II Samuel 5). Words of condemnation upon this ancient enemy would be welcomed by Israel.

Amos began his pronouncement of judgment by using Gaza as representative of the entire nation of Philistia. Gaza was the southernmost of the cities of Philistia and was important because of its commerce and its location as the last Philistine city on the way to Egypt.

Like Syria, the Philistines were guilty of "three transgressions . . . yea, . . . four." Their "climax sin" was a wholesale trafficking in slavery. They had carried into exile a whole people, to hand them over to Edom (1:6). That is, they took the aged men, the women, and the children. They did not have enough respect for human personality to spare the helpless. Slavery was not a secondary aspect of war with them; it was a primary means of acquiring revenue. They raided for the sole purpose of acquiring slaves rather than defending their border or aiding an ally.

After acquiring the slaves, the Philistines handed them over to Edom, who, in all likelihood, served as the middleman in bartering in the lives of men. Edom would, in turn, pass the slaves on to an interested buyer for a price. According to Amos, such practices would not escape the judgment of Yahweh.

A "fire" would be sent upon the Philistines. The devastation of war would come upon them in repeated blows. Her walls would be destroyed, and her dwellings built out of the revenues from her slavery business would be devoured. The inhabitants of Ashdod, a strong fortification between Gaza and Joppa, would be cut off (destroyed) in the calamity of war. The ruler of Ashkelon, a city midway between Ashdod and Gaza, would be cut off by destruction. Ekron, located some dozen miles north and east of Ashhdod, would experience judgment at the hand of Yahweh. In addition, any persons surviving in other areas of Philistia would perish in a subsequent judgment.

Upon the completion of the statement of condemnation of the Philistines there must have been an air of resounding approval. This was exactly what Israel thought the Philistines deserved. They were delighted with the prospects of their destruction.

The judgment referred to, though not specified, may have been that wrought by the Assyrians. Tiglath Pileser III attacked Gaza in 734 B.C. and exacted tribute. In 711 B.C., on account of her refusal to meet the tribute demands of Assyria, Ashdod was destroyed and the citizens taken into exile. Finally, a few years later (701 B.C.) Ekron and Ashkelon joined in revolt and were severely chastised by Sennacherib.

3. *Judgment upon Tyre* (1:9, 10). Amos turned next to Tyre, Israel's neighbor to the north and west. Tyre most likely represents the Phoenician nation; yet Tyre was in her own right a significant part of the Phoenician country. The city was famous because of its harbors and trade as well as its size (see Ezekiel 28). Like many nations before and since, the character of the principal city becomes the character of the nation. For this reason, if for no other, it could have represented the entire nation.

The people of Tyre (Phoenicia) were condemned "because they handed over a whole people as captives to Edom." Here it would seem that Phoenicia had assumed the roll of middleman. They were not charged with taking captives, but for acting as slave traders or slave agents, and they did so despite a "covenant of brotherhood." That is, they acted in an unbrotherly way and did so despite a prior agreement (covenant) not to.

In I Kings 5:2ff., there is mention of a covenant between Hiram and Solomon which may have contained a clause in which Phoenicia agreed not to barter in Hebrew slaves. If such were the case, this would explain the condemnation by the prophet. Some, on the other hand, suggest that the covenant referred to was one existing between the Phoenicians in which they agreed not to barter in Phoenician lives. In either event, it condemns untrustworthiness and infidelity in keeping a covenant as well as the heartlessness of bartering in human life.

The guilty nation would be subjected to the ravages of war. Tyre would be destroyed and the people punished for their unbrotherly conduct. How the judgment referred to was specifically carried out is unknown. It may have come through the hands of the Assyrians, who exacted tribute and finally in 664 B.C. overwhelmed the city under the leadership of Ashur-banapal, or it may refer to the greatest disaster to befall Tyre — that of Alexander the Great in 332 B.C., an assault which resulted in the death of multitudes and the enslavement of thousands.

If the sin of the people of Tyre was in the selling of Hebrews into slavery or even their own brothers with whom they had covenanted not to, one can readily see the reaction of Israel to the words of condemnation by Amos. Another of her enemies was brought under the condemning voice of the prophet. In this they were delighted.

4. *Judgment upon Edom* (1:11, 12). By turning to Edom, Amos continued the procedure of circumscribing Israel. This time judgment was pronounced upon the descendants of Esau located to the south and east of Israel. The hostility between Israel and Edom was traced by biblical writers back to the birth of Jacob and Esau (Genesis 25ff.). This continued hostility may have been the basis of Edom's refusal of passage to Israel as she pressed on to Canaan (Numbers 20) as well as the basis of Edom's attitude at the time of the destruction of Jerusalem (Obadiah 10-14).

The specific condemnation of Edom, set against the background of three transgressions, was because he "pursued his brother with the sword, and did cast off all pity, and his anger did tear perpetually, and he kept his wrath forever." He "pursued" (as the hungry his prey) not his enemy but his brother (Israel), whom he now treated as an enemy. He pursued him until he could deliver a telling and cruel blow. Such pursuit of a brother was possible only because of the smothering of every motive and occasion for compassion; that is, Edom "cast off all pity." Pity was stifled because he "kept his anger perpetually";

that is, he did not allow relationship or mercy to temper or dissipate his anger. It continued in burst after burst, and because "he kept his wrath for ever," he did not allow time to do its healing work. Nothing under such conditions could effect a change in his attitude of hostility and animosity. Therefore, judgment, "a fire" (the ravages of war) would befall Teman. Teman was a district in the north of Edom and in the present usage seems to have represented the nation as specific cities have done in the previous judgments. The devastation would also devour the palaces (the dwellings of the leaders) of Bozrah, one of the chief cities of the nation. The nation would be devastated by an enemy who would appear in the due season.

Such long-standing and deep-seated hostility must have been the bane of every Israelite. To hear Amos pronounce judgment on those who had kept their animosity and vengeance alive for so many centuries was a welcome sound to their ears. Amos, so far as Israel was concerned, was preaching better and better all the time.

The fulfillment of Edom's judgment, though not stated, was most likely realized in oppression by the Assyrians, who listed the Edomites among their oppressed peoples, or by the Babylonians (Jeremiah 27:3ff.), who succeeded the Assyrians as a world power.

5: *Judgment upon Ammon* (1:13-15). Amos moved next to the east of Israel as he turned to Ammon. The relationship of Ammon and Israel extended back to the period of the Judges, when Ammon joined with Moab and Amalek to smite Israel (Judges 3:12ff.) and occupied at least a portion of Israel (Judges 11:12). Later, because of the continued enmity between Israel and Ammon, Saul engaged them and destroyed their forces (I Samuel 11:11). These two events and others later in their history (II Kings 24:2; Jeremiah 40:14) would have provided sufficient grounds for an unfriendly, even hostile, relationship between Israel and Ammon.

The "climax sin" in the case of the Ammonites was their attempt to "enlarge their border" and the inhumanity associated with it.

Ammon had engaged in military activity not for self-defense but "that they might enlarge their border," that is, that they might satisfy their appetites for more and more territory. In attempting to acquire greater territorial control, they were resorting to extreme cruelty. They were respecting no one. Life was cheap and expendable for them. Life was of such little worth to them that they would, upon coming upon a pregnant and defenseless woman, rip open her body that she and her unborn child might die. This was the apex of cruelty. Whether it was a practice resulting from greed for possession alone, as the text seems to imply, or as some believe an act to keep the population from rebuilding, it was an inhumanity which no one could tolerate. Certainly no prophet could remain silent. Amos, therefore, pronounced judgment, "a fire" (the ravages of war), upon Ammon: "The fire" would fall upon the wall of Rabbah, the capital city, which represented the nation, and her palaces would be destroyed by the "shouting" victors, who had become the instruments of judgment. The enemy armies would fall upon Ammon as "a storm" — "a tempest"; that is, they would devastate the land, capture their nobles and exile them as swiftly, as decisively, and as completely as a tornado or hurricane would a bundle of straw.

On account of Ammon's unfriendly relationships with Israel and their extreme inhumanity, all Israel would have been pleased with Amos' speaking these words of judgment upon them. Not having noticed that Amos was slowly but surely weaving a web in which to ensnare Israel in her own guilt, his hearers continued to find satisfaction in the oracles of this preacher of righteousness.

The fulfillment of judgment upon Ammon is more difficult to seek to determine than some of the others. But, as in the case of several of the other neighbors of Israel, Babylonia may have been the nation responsible for dealing the blow. Whether this was so or not, the Babylonians do list them as tribute payers.

6. *Judgment upon Moab* (2:1-3). To the south and east of Israel lay Moab. From the time of the Judges when Eglon smote

Israel (Judges 3:12 ff.), there were strained relationships between the Israelites and the Moabites. During the reign of Saul it is stated that "he fought against all his enemies on every side" (I Samuel 14:47 ff.). One of the enemies was Moab. Still later David made Moab his servant and required tribute of them (II Samuel 8:2). These incidents would explain any satisfaction Israel would have had in the words of Amos, but beyond these events were other factors.

The present wickedness of Moab, against the background of three transgressions, was that "he burned the bones of the king of Edom into lime." There are two general explanations of this evil. There are those who suggest that though there was no clear concept of the after-life at this point, there was the belief in some sort of quasi-existence. This quasi-existence was related to the body of the deceased. There was an unexplained relation between the body and continued existence. To destroy the body was to deny any existence at all beyond the veil of death. On the other hand, the sin of the Moabites was in all probability simply the desecration of the king's grave, a desecration motivated by relentless hatred for Edom and its ruler. Either of these would have provoked words of judgment from a prophet of Yahweh.

The judgment pronounced was "a fire." The "fire" would devour the palaces (the dwellings of the nobles and princes) of Kerioth. Kerioth was a great Moabitish city, located in the tableland of Moab, which may be identified with Ar, the capital. The impending destruction would bring chaos and confusion ("uproar") into the life of Moab. The "uproar" would be created by "the sound of the trumpet," that is, the bugle sound of advance as the destructive forces marched against Moab. The enemy would cut off — both king (chieftain) and princes — in the destruction which was drawing near; that is, their leaders would be destroyed.

If hostility between Israel and Moab had persisted through the years, then there is reason to believe that here as in the other judgment statements there was a genuine rejoicing by those who heard the prophet condemn the Moabites. Should the hostility between Israel and Moab have subsided, there would have remained the feeling that one who desecrates the grave, even of an enemy, deserves condemnation. In either case, the words of Amos would have pleased his hearers.

There is no extant evidence of any destruction coinciding with this announcement of the prophet. In all likelihood the destruction was the work of the Babylonians because they do list the Moabites in their monuments. Beyond this there seems to be little evidence to consider.

7. *Judgment upon Judah* (2:4, 5). Amos wove a web around the east, the north, and the west sides of Israel. Then he turned to his own nation Judah on the south and in doing so completely circumscribed Israel. Perhaps Amos saved Judah for this time because there would have been those in Israel who felt a sympathy for her even though hostility had existed from the time of the division (I Kings 15:7; II Kings 9:24ff.; 14:12ff.). To have considered Judah earlier, therefore, might have interfered with his scheme for circumscribing Israel.

Judah's "crowning sin" was in the rejection of the law of Yahweh and in turning to the idols of Canaan. In rejecting "the instruction of the Lord," they were rejecting the written and spoken law which Israel had received through their spiritual leaders. They had refused to keep "his statutes," that is, the religious, moral and civil law of Yahweh. They had, instead, turned to their "lies," that is, their false gods. In doing so they had spurned the true help offered them by the God who brought them out of Egypt. It was a spurning of the law which was no new thing with the present generation but one which had been practiced by their fathers and thereby taught their children. The children had gone the way "after which their fathers walked."

The sin of Judah calls for "a fire." The ravages of war would destroy the palaces (the dwellings) of the nobles and the wealthy of the day. A word like that would have been a welcome sound to the ears of many, especially those who had been the brunt of the abuse of the nobility and the rich. The fact that Jerusalem would suffer in the destruction would not have deterred such a feeling; for after all, they had their own centers at which to worship. They had been getting on without the Holy City; surely they could continue to do so.

Though the circumstances of the judgment of Judah referred to by Amos are not specifically stated, they may have included the siege by Sennacherib (II Kings 18:13ff.) and the siege by Nebuchadnezzar in 597 B.C. (II Kings 24:8ff.). Whether these were included or not is unknown. Yet even if they were not, there would seem to be little doubt that the ultimate realization of the judgment was in the destruction of Jerusalem in 586 B.C. by the forces of Babylon (II Kings 25:8,9).

With Judah added to his list of those subject to judgment, Amos had circumscribed Israel. There would have been little disputing among themselves that the nations deserved the judgment announced by the prophet. Surely the wickedness of those surrounding Israel deserved punishment; with this most of Amos' hearers would agree. The web was now tightly woven around Israel. She alone had escaped the prophet's words of condemnation. If these words had come to be known abroad in the land, there must have been a growing interest in who would be next. They would not have to wait long to see.

8. *Judgment upon Israel* (2:6-8). After so circuitous a route, after having carefully woven the web, Amos turned to Israel and called for self-evaluation and self-condemnation — the last and most difficult of all human enterprises. "For three transgressions of Israel, . . . for four" brings the prophet to the heart of the matter. The neighbors of Israel had sinned, yes, but so had Israel. Israel's sins were many and were at least as deserving of judgment as the others. In fact, Israel, a covenant nation, should have known better than the others with the exception of Judah who was a covenant nation also; therefore, they were, if anything, more deserving of punishment than those outside the covenant.

"They"—the leaders, the wealthy, the powerful—"have sold the innocent for silver"; that is, they have been engaging in the practice of selling judgment, unjust judgments against the innocent for a price ("silver"), that is, judgments at the court of law were being bought and sold (compare Isaiah 1:23; Micah 3:9). The conditions were such that a man could buy any court decision he wished for a price. If the price — "silver" — refers to the smallest silver money piece, as suggested by some, then it magnifies the tragic level of their injustice. For little or nothing a man could buy a decision in his favor regardless of his own guilt or the innocence of the other party. On the other hand, recent commentators suggest that this is nothing more than a reference to the selling of slaves. Perhaps both were involved in the conditions of Israel.

Amos continued his indictment by declaring that "they sold . . . the needy for a pair of shoes." This evil may mean that they sold a man — a poor man pressed under obligations, hard put at the moment — into slavery for the price of his obligation. In other words, if a man had a debt for a pair of shoes and could not meet the due date, he would be sold into slavery for the price of his indebtedness. On the other hand, the statement may refer to a practice of selling men into slavery for a mere pittance. In either case, it was an expression of greed, wanton heartlessness, and disrespect for mankind. It could not go unnoticed. It could not be ignored by a prophet such as Amos.

Israel was also condemned for trampling "upon the heads of the poor" (2:7) and thrusting "aside the meek from the way." The powerful and influential of the land could hardly wait to see the poor and innocent ("humble") in mourning because of impoverished circumstances which had been caused by their injustices and unconcern.

But that was not all. Israel had succumbed to the practices of the fertility cult and the resultant temple prostitution (2:7b). They were thoughtlessly using in their carnal practices "the garments taken in pledge" (2:8a), that is, garments taken in pledge on an obligation which were to be returned at sundown each day for protection from the cold of night (Exodus 22:26). They did not for a moment consider the welfare of the poor man who had been denied the protection of his wrap. He was their least and last concern.

Finally, Amos decried the drinking of wine bought by monies acquired through the illegal "sale of justice" by the judges. This indulgence was being carried on in connection with a corrupted religious practice (2:8b) which was foreign to the practice of Mosaic religion.

These words must have caused a deep silence to fall over Amos' hearers. Hostility must have shown in the faces of many. Resentment must have been evident, but Amos had not finished. He continued to press the matter by pointing to the real implications of what had happened in the life of the nation. Something more than injustice, apostasy, and immorality were there. There was an unthinkable ingratitude which expressed itself in what they had done.

9. *The Ingratitude of Israel* (2:9-12). How could a nation, so providentially provided for and cared for, do as Israel had done? How could a people with such guideposts go so far against the will and purpose of God? How could a nation for whom God had done so much do so little of what He asked of them in return? In coming to grips with the problem Amos turned to a consideration of what God had done for Israel.

First, He made possible the destruction of the Amorites. The Amorites were the pre-Israelitish population west of the Jordan. They had been overthrown with the assistance of God. Despite their height and their strength they had nevertheless fallen before the forces of Israel. Their fruit (prosperity) and roots (source of life) had been destroyed; that is, they had been completely overcome (2:9). God had destroyed the invincible occupants of Canaan and brought Israel in to occupy that land. The Israelites had been able to conquer, not in their own strength, but through the help of God.

Next, Amos pointed to the fact that Yahweh had overthrown the Egyptians, brought Israel out of bondage, cared for them through the long period of wandering in the wilderness (2:10).

These mighty works which were associated with the Exodus stood out beyond all other events in Israel's history. Implicit in this verse are those factors which formed the basis of the faith of Israel. The first of these was God's election of Israel to be a peculiar people with the responsiblity of following through with His purpose in Abraham to be a blessing to all mankind. Second, He had led them into the wilderness and through it. During the journey He provided for their material needs, but at Sinai He entered into covenant relationship with them and gave them the law as its basis. He committed Himself to be their God if they would be His people. If Israel would trust Yahweh and obey the law which he had given them, the covenant relationship would remain. He would be theirs, and they would be His. The third act of God in Amos' account of the Exodus was in Yahweh's support of Israel in the conquest of the Amorites, which has been referred to earlier. This was an accomplishment which the Israelites could never have realized through their own strength and ingenuity because their knowledge of warfare, as well as their equipment to carry it on, was seriously lacking. Therefore, their victory was realized by the help of Yahweh on their behalf — He had made possible their triumph.

In calling these incidents to their attention once again, Amos was but implying that as God had been with the nation in the past as it had faced need, He would be with it now provided its people would look to Him in trust and obedience. Though the needs of Israel may have changed, the God of Israel had not.

The last thing Amos called to their attention was the fact that God had considered their spiritual needs and had given them the prophets, who rendered great service to Israel by their preaching which kept conscience alive, and the Nazarites, who served the nation as examples in consecration (2:11). Since man is a spiritual being, he must have spiritual counsel and guidance. The prophets and Nazarites were the instruments given Israel to counsel and guide her. The prophet was called and commissioned to speak for God. His message was to keep Israel faithful to the purpose which God had in choosing her. The

Nazarite, who abstained from all intoxicants, unclean food, the cutting of his hair (a sign of consecration), and any contact with the dead, provided Israel with an ideal of consecration. To belong to God meant to abstain from the world. This was a challenge Israel would need all her days. God had provided it in the Nazarites.

Following these statements describing God's providential care for Israel, God through Amos raised the question, "Is this not so, O Israelites? Is it not so that God has done these things for Israel?" The answer must be "yes!" In the light of the required response, the implicit question faced by the nation was, "But what have you done in return?" It was a question which could not go unanswered. Amos attempted the answer by saying, "The Nazarites were given you to keep you mindful of the need for resisting the claims of worldliness, the need for staying with the proper traditions; but you insisted they compromise themselves. The prophets were given to keep conscience alive, but you commanded them to be silent. Thus you did away with the guideposts erected by God to keep you from worldliness and injustice. Therefore, judgment must fall upon such a sinful nation."

10. *The Effect of Israel's Transgression — Judgment* (2:13-16). As a result of the transgression of Israel, God will come in judgment — His judgment is sure. The concept in 2:13, somewhat difficult, seems to suggest the relationship of God to the transgression of Israel. Either the sin of Israel was pressing down upon God, or God was about to press down upon Israel as a loaded wagon would press upon any object beneath its wheels. Whichever the case, the results are the same. Crushing judgment will befall the nation of evildoers.

When the judgment comes, those within Israel will not escape. Even the fleetest warrior will be unable to flee (2:14a). The "strong shall not exert his strength." On account of the horrors witnessed he will not have the strength of heart to gather his strength to do battle or escape (2:14b). "The warrior," the man recognized and revered for his courage, "shall not save himself" (2:14c). The man who handles the bow, the one who is swift of foot, as well as the one riding upon the horse, shall not be able to deliver himself (2:15). When the judgment comes, the courageous man among the mighty "shall flee away naked"; that is, he shall throw his weapons to the wind and seek to flee the terror which has befallen him (2:16). The judgment will fall upon the mighty as well as upon the weak, and none will escape no matter the nature of their resources.

Having come to the heart of the matter by slowly weaving a web around Israel, Amos declared that Israel would be judged just as the other nations had been. He suggested that she was as guilty as the remainder of the nations and perhaps intended to imply that she was even more guilty. God had done much for Israel in destroying the Amorites, in leading her out of Egypt as well as through the desert, and in giving her both prophet and Nazarite. Yet in spite of all that He had done, Israel had rejected God's plan and purpose for her life. In light of this, nothing but judgment awaited her. All her gain would be loss. What a tragic waste in human life and noble purpose! This was the tragic story of a nation who knew the high and noble purposes of God but who cast them aside in quest of personal gain and pleasure.

The fulfillment of these pronouncements of judgment, though not given by the prophet, must have been ultimately realized in the devastation of Israel by the Assyrians. Shalmaneser (727-822 B.C.), the king of Assyria, besieged Samaria three years and died. The pursuit was continued and concluded by his successor, Sargon II (722-705 B.C.), who had the event recorded in his annals where he calls attention to the fact that in his first year of reign he besieged and captured Samaria. Thus the judgment pronounced by the prophet came to be realized in history.

Having concluded the discussion of the sins of the nations and shown the ingratitude of Israel for all Yahweh had done for her in the Exodus as well as the effect of Israel's transgression, Amos turned to expand his message. He began by calling attention to the responsibility of station.

FOR FURTHER STUDY

1. Read the articles in ZPBD or IDB on "Damascus," I, 757, 758; "Philistines," III, 791-795; "Phoenicia," III, 800-805; "Edom," II, 24-26; "Ammon," I, 108-114; "Moab," III, 409-419; "Amorites," I, 115-116; and "Nazarites," III, 526, 527 or in some Bible Dictionary.
2. List the "crowning sins" in each of the nations mentioned in Amos. Have men and nations changed? Discuss.
3. What positive effects may be learned from Amos' approach to the sins of Israel as one comes to deal with the sins of his own society?
4. What providences have been recognized as the acts of God in the history of your nation? What are the modern attitudes toward these? Why? How may any worthy attitude be secured and maintained?
5. What evidences of ingratitude may be found in modern society?

CHAPTER 3

THE RESPONSIBILITY OF STATION
(Amos 3:1-8)

1. Israel, a Privileged Nation (3:2a)
2. The Peril of Privilege (3:2b)
3. The Principle of Cause and Effect (3:3-6)

Chapter 3 begins a section, including chapters 3 - 6, which in large measure expands what Amos has already said concerning Israel in the roll call of the nations (2:6-16). There he dealt with the wickedness within Israel (2:6-8), the providences of God for Israel (2:9-12), and the certain judgment to come upon Israel (2:13-16). Here he deals with basically the same material but on an expanded scale and in a different sequence.

An admonition to listen begins this section. It was an admonition from God, addressed to both Judah and Israel, but primarily to Israel. It involved their past, their present, and their future and was predicated upon Israel's relationship to God.

1. *Israel, a Privileged Nation* (3:2a). Throughout her history, Israel thought of herself as a privileged nation. It was a concept based upon the fact that of all the nations of the earth she alone had been elected as a special instrument in God's eternal purpose. The concept was initiated in God's call of Abraham (Genesis 12:1-3).

With the call of Abraham, he and his descendants were to be a source of blessing to all mankind (Genesis 12:1-3); that is, all nations would be blessed through the revelation given to Abraham and the nation born as his seed. In light of their role, God committed Himself to bless both Abraham and His seed in

39

their mission. Their names would be above every name (Genesis 12:2), and their enemies would be thwarted by the curse of God (Genesis 12:3). Such a commission and such a promise strongly implied a privilege role as well as a unique relationship.

God's call to Abraham, and in that, His call to his descendants was not to be forgotten. It was not even forgotten during the long years of Egyptian bondage. This was evidenced as God began to deal with Abraham's descendants, who had been in bondage for such a long time. The basis of God's approach to Israel in Egypt was the ancient pledge He had made to Abraham and his descendants (Exodus 6:2ff.).

In order that His pledge to Abraham might be kept, God would deliver Israel from the bondage of Egypt. They were to be the first redeemed of the ages. Their deliverance would become the most significant event in the history of Abraham's seed. The deliverance from Egypt re-emphasized for the nation that God's purpose for Abraham had now become His purpose for it. As God had called Abraham out of Ur, He had now called His descendants (Israel) out of Egypt for the same purpose (Exodus 19:5, 6). No other nation had known such a privileged station nor fallen to so grave a responsibility.

The privileges enjoyed by Israel because of her relationship to God at the Exodus became a consideration for every age. From the time of Moses on, the Exodus became the principal basis for all future relationships between God and Israel. It was as though the purpose which God had revealed to Abraham had been absorbed in the larger purpose for the nation. Therefore, when Amos began to deal with the burden of his ministry, it was not strange that he should discuss the privilege known by Israel as a result of the Exodus.

This great privilege expressed itself in the prophet's statement, "You only have I known of all the families of the earth" (3:2). Before we discuss this clause, it is interesting to note the close relationship between it and the one in the preceding verse, "which I brought up out of the land of Egypt" (3:1). This relationship suggests that the Exodus was now the primary factor in the closeness of God and Israel; that is, the call of

Abraham and his descendants had not been superseded by the Exodus but had in reality been reiterated and reaffirmed on a national basis rather than a family basis.

The statement, "you only have I known of all the families of the earth . . . " placed Israel in a place of special privilege. The word *known* used by the prophet suggests an intimacy comparable to that known in the marital relationship. It declares that God knew Israel as He knew no other nation, that He purposed for her as He had purposed for no other people. She was to be the avenue through which God would reveal Himself and His purpose for all mankind. The word *known* also implies that Israel knew God in a special way. No other nation had ever experienced the Exodus; no other nation had ever entered into covenant with God; no other nation had ever been given a land "flowing with milk and honey." Israel was indeed a nation of privilege. God knew her in a significant way, but she also knew God in a unique way.

In the covenant which God made with Israel, He revealed to her His will and purpose. He had given her the law, which consisted of the words of the covenant, that she might worship Him, serve Him and reveal His nature and purpose to the nations of the earth. Israel had been elected and given this lofty station of privilege that she might be used of God to bless all men. This one fact created a peril for the chosen nation.

2. *The Peril of Privilege* (3:2b). Israel, the chosen nation, faced the temptation which besets the privileged of every generation, that is, a tendency on the part of those who are privileged to ignore or neglect the responsibility which inevitably follows it. This tendency expresses itself in three ways. First, those of privilege frequently interpret the advantages of their station as a personal favor or blessing to be used for their own individual pleasure and profit. Second, the privileged tend to consider themselves better, more worthy and more deserving than others. This often causes a loss of interest in and concern for the less fortunate and needy. Third, the privileged interpret their status as one which places them above and beyond the laws of responsibility and judgment.

The nation not only faced the temptation of this tendency; they yielded to it. They reasoned that the blessings of God were for personal enjoyment; therefore, they were "not grieved for the afflictions of Joseph" (6:6c). They believed themselves to be of greater value to God than the other nations of the earth because of their election (3:2a). They considered that their election set them outside the reach of God's judgment (9:10). Amos disagreed with their deductions. He contended that, if anything, they were more responsible than the others because of their knowledge of God and His purpose for them.

The attitude of the prophet was revealed in the words, "Therefore, I will visit upon you all your iniquities" (3:2b). These words suggest the peril of privilege. Those chosen of God are, because of His choosing, placed under grave responsibility. This point was made in the use of "therefore." Israel, having been elected by God, known by Him, was responsible, therefore, for her response to that privilege. Since Israel was known of God, she was responsible to God. She was responsible for "all" she was and all she did. Every deviation from the true, the right, and the good would make her subject to judgment (3:2b).

The words of Amos concerning the iniquities of Israel suggest the ominous thought that privilege is fraught with danger. One danger is that the privileged will not measure up to the responsibility implied by privilege. Another danger is that the privileged will be judged as a result of their failure. Both dangers were real to Israel. In fact, Amos suggested in the words, "Therefore, I will visit upon you all your iniquities," that they had not only failed in responsibility, but they were also on the way to judgment. All their iniquities would be visited with judgment.

3. *The Principle of Cause and Effect* (3:3-6). After the declaration that Israel would be visited in judgment, the prophet doubtless faced the questionings of his audience. Implied in his defense of this message by the use of the principle of cause and effect was a skepticism on the part of those who listened. They not only doubted that the words of Amos were valid; they doubted that he himself was a bona fide messenger of God. He

sought to convince them by the use of the principle of cause
and effect.

(1) The first illustration used by the prophet was that of the
journey of two men (3:3). The question, "Shall two walk together, except they have agreed?" suggests that the reason for
their walking together was that they were in agreement. Those
who heard the prophet knew of the dangers of the highways of
that day. Therefore, a man would not travel alone if he could
avoid it. Yet, rather than join with a stranger who might become his robber, he would go on alone. So, to see two men
journeying together suggested that they had met by appointment and were in agreement and accord. The same principle
was implied when a prophet spoke the word of God. It meant
that they were of one mind and purpose. To be so minded suggests that they were walking together. The prophet spoke because he and God were together in mind and purpose.

(2) The second illustration was the roar of the lion (3:4). The
first question raised about the lion suggests that it did not roar
before it leaped upon its prey. When one heard a lion's roar,
he understood that the lion had already sprung from his lying
in wait. The second question suggests that the young lion does
not growl before the food is brought to the lair. He growls when
he settles down to his meal.

(3) The third illustration had to do with a trap (3:5). If a bird
were to fall to the earth, it was because a trap had been set.
Should a trap spring up, it was evident that something had
sprung it. Birds do not fall nor do traps spring without cause.

(4) The fourth illustration dealt with the signalling of and approach of danger to a city (3:6). When men heard the peal of
a trumpet, they knew danger was near. If disaster befell a city,
men knew God was the source of it (3:6b).

With these four illustrations before those who may have
questioned him, Amos prepared to apply them by stating that
"the Lord Yahweh will do nothing except he reveal his secret
unto his servants the prophets" (3:7). The "secret" was the
purpose or plan of God. The prophet was declaring that crises
did not come without the prior appearance of a messenger to

bring a warning of its approach. Then he made the application.

Since God was active in the world, certain effects were inevitable. For the prophet to proclaim the Word of the Lord meant that he and Yahweh were in accord. He was, in fact, proclaiming the truth because they were walking together. God's message had become Amos' message and Amos would have no message without the company — "walking together" — of God. The next result of the principle of cause and effect was in the roar of the lion (3:8a). The roar was the roar of Yahweh. Its first result was in inciting fear. The roar meant destruction was already upon them. There was no escape. The second result was upon the prophet. Having heard the roar and knowing its meaning, he could do no less than prophesy (3:8b).

Herein Amos was saying that his words were as surely related to the principle of cause and effect as any point illustrated. He prophesied because the "lion" had roared, because "the Lord Yahweh hath spoken." He could not, in fact, have done otherwise. To have done otherwise would have been as unreasonable as two walking together without appointment — or a lion roaring without a prey — or a bird falling without a snare — or a trap springing without a prey — or a trumpet being blown without an enemy — or a city falling without God having done it. Such things just did not happen, nor did a prophet prophesy when he had not heard God's voice. On the other hand, when he had heard God's voice, he could do nothing less than prophesy (3:8).

FOR FURTHER STUDY

1. For the Egyptian background which relates to Israel read *A History of Egypt* by James Breasted.
2. For a discussion of "The Exodus" read pp. 53-67 in *Biblical Archaeology* by G. E. Wright.
3. What factors in the founding of America seem to parallel those in the founding of Israel? What part did God play in both?

4. What perils are associated with the privileges enjoyed in the abundance of our own society?
5. List the iniquities in your own community. What can be done to correct them?
6. In light of Amos' statement that Israel would be visited in judgment because of iniquity, what implications are contained therein for present society?
7. What are some of the bases for determining whether the modern prophet has been sent from God? Is the principle of cause and effect still a valid principle? Discuss.

CHAPTER 4

AN INVITATION TO RUIN
(Amos 3:9-15)

1. The Conditions Within Israel (3:9, 10)
2. An Invitation Accepted (3:11a)
3. The Consequences of the Anniversary (3:11b-15)

Having called Israel's attention to her place of privilege, her resultant responsibility, and the certainty of her iniquities being visited upon them, Amos turned to describe these iniquities. After having done so, he revealed that they would result in the judgment and destruction of the nation and its institutions.

1. *The Conditions Within Israel* (3:9, 10). In 3:9, 10 Amos turned to an added description of Israel's iniquity. He began by summoning the nations, who had been Israel's enemies and who lived by different standards, to assemble and observe the confusion which resulted when a nation with the highest standards did not practice them.

First, Amos pointed toward the oppression found within Samaria (the nation, 3:9). It was oppression created by those (the powerful, wealthy, ruling class) bent on personal gain. They had "overturned" justice by ignoring or setting aside every standard required by it and human sympathy. They engaged in extortion, bribery, unfair business practices, and excessive taxation. They were guilty of storing "up violence and robbery in their palaces"; that is, that which they accumulated or acquired they secured through violence and robbery (3:10b). They had built and furnished their winter palaces and their summer palaces from the resources of robbery and oppression practiced upon their lesser or weaker neighbors. This had

47

brought about a breach in society. The city and the nation were filled with disorders. Chaos was abroad in the land (3:9b). It had resulted from the miscarriage of justice at the hands of those responsible for its continued existence (3:10b).

After having specified particular evils, the prophet summarized their condition by saying, "They know not to do right" (3:10a). It was as though the prophet were suggesting that it had been a thing of long standing. It had gone on over such an extended period of time that "they" had lost all sense of the right — the straight. "They" refers to those who occupied the mansions and the palaces. "They" made up the real social and civil authority. "They" were the responsible leaders. Yet, instead of upholding right and law as the responsible should, "they" had dedicated themselves, by their attitudes as well as their practices, to its very destruction. Having followed these practices so long, they had lost every sense of right as well as the will to defend and practice it. They had forgotten the truth of the writer of Proverbs: "Better is little, with the fear of Jehovah, than great treasures and trouble therewith" (15:16).

Such conduct not only brought about a disintegration of the social structure, it also called for judgment. It issued its own invitation to destruction. To defy the principles of justice, equity, and fairness and to employ practices and methods which would render justice inoperative was an invitation to ruin. Such an invitation, consciously or unconsciously, had been extended by Israel in both attitude and action.

2. *An Invitation Accepted* (3:11a). To engage in injustice as Israel had done could not escape the attention and the judgment of the righteous God of Israel. This they knew. It was not as though they were without knowledge. In light of their knowledge, then, the thing which was about to befall the nation was of their own choosing. God had told the people that their iniquity would be visited upon them (3:2). Nevertheless they went on as though they had not been warned. To have done so was to court and invite disaster. When it came, it would take the form of an adversary, a nation powerful and destructive (3:11a). The

appearance of that nation would bring ruin and loss to all acquired through their iniquitous practices. All their strength,
all their resources, all their fortifications, and all their treasures
would be affected as a result of their iniquity (3:11b).

The invitation for a divine visitation which Israel had extended through her failure or refusal to abide by the laws and
standards of God had been accepted. Judgment was on its way.
The nation was sure to suffer when it arrived.

3. *The Consequence of the Adversary* (3:11b-15). The
losses to be sustained by the nation as a result of the adversary
were to reach every area of its life. The judgment would have
an effect upon every aspect of national life. Its security would
be affected (3:11). Its defenses (its walls and fortifications)
upon which the nation had depended for security would be destroyed. The adversary was capable of such destructiveness
that defenses would not deter him. Dwellings (memorials to injustice and oppression) where violence had been stored would
be plundered and pillaged (3:11, 15). Here it becomes obvious
that the prophet's condemnation was directed toward the nobles
and leaders of the land who had tolerated injustice and had
themselves exploited the weaker citizens of the state. Amos was
speaking primarily to those living in luxury, splendor, and ease
(3:12b).

The destruction, when it did come, would be of such scope
that only a small segment of the nation would escape. In dealing with this point the prophet would seem to be answering
the question, "How severe will the destruction be?" Amos announced that it would be comparable to a lion pouncing upon
a lamb and consuming all but "two leg bones or a piece of an
ear" (3:12). As the lion would leave a few small fragments, so
would the lion who roared from Jerusalem leave a mere handful of the inhabitants of Samaria. Those who had involved
themselves in the thoughtless practices of a nation, those who
should have known better and acted differently would sustain
the severest kind of destruction.

It is interesting to note that Amos included "the church" in

his pronouncement of judgment. He revealed that in the day
that God visited Israel in judgment he would "also visit the altars
of Bethel; and the horns of the altar shall be cut off, and fall to
the ground" (3:14b). The safety once afforded or that which
was believed to have been afforded by the religious establishment would also come under judgment and would therefore no
longer provide "the security" which would have ordinarily been
found there. The "horns of the altar" were the extended corners
of the altar — pointed projections at each corner, which may
have suggested the appearance of an attempt to contain something (Leviticus 4:7, 18, 30). Since the altar was an evidence
of the presence of God, the horns may have been there to symbolize the containment of His presence or even the containment
of the offering. Whether this was so or not, it is known that
the horns represented the most sacred point of the altar. Too,
they marked out the point at which a fugitive could find security.

As far as the horns being a point of security, a fugitive could
claim asylum by racing to the altar where he would find deliverance until those responsible for justice could decide his innocence or guilt (I Kings 1:50 ff.). If, then, the horns of the altar
were to be cut off in the judgment, it must have been for the
purpose of emphasizing the fact that there would be no place
for the fugitive of Israel to escape. This fact may suggest that
their guilt was so obvious that the question of their guilt or innocence need not be dealt with. So the horns of the altar were
to be cut off. Even the altar which signified God's presence was
gone. Israel was now without recourse. The judgment of God
would fall, and any security she may have found in the presence
of the horns of the altar would avail nothing. That which Israel
had sown she would reap. She had predetermined her own end
by her unrighteousness. There would be no security left for her.
Having sown in unrighteousness and injustice, she had invited
her own ruin, and nothing would now turn it back. Her luxurious
palaces erected from the revenues of violence and robbery would
perish along with the religion which had permitted and even
encouraged such practices.

FOR FURTHER STUDY

1. Read the articles in ZPBD and IDB on "Samaria," IV, 182-188 and "Bethel," I, 391-393.
2. Read the article on "Altar" in ZPBD and IDB, I, 96-100 and in *Ancient Israel* by R. de Vaux, 406-414.
3. Name some of the conditions produced by injustice in the life of the nations of the world.
4. List the conditions in Israel which were summarized in the statement, "For they know not to do right . . . "
5. What conditions in modern society suggest the use of the statement by the modern prophet? What can be done to bring a change? Discuss.
6. What factors went into the tragedy of Old Testament Church? Was Amos dealing with this issue as he spoke of the destruction of the altar? What seems to be the inevitable result when a church fails to have a positive effect upon the society which it serves?

CHAPTER 5

THE SIGNS OF THE TIMES
(Amos 4:1-13)

1. The Major Premise (4:2, 3)
2. The Circumstances of the Day (4:1, 4-11)
3. Preparation for Judgment (4:12)
4. The God They Will Meet (4:13)

After having declared the basis and degree of punishment provoked by the conditions within Israel, Amos continued to delve into the sins of the nation. Sin after sin was added to those already described. These additions seemed to eliminate every possibility of escape. They revealed the true character of the nation. Their pretense would be exposed. The patience of God was shown to be exhausted. Israel had to face imminent disaster. The signs demanded it.

1. *The Major Premise* (4:2, 3). The major premise back of all the prophet had said and all that he would speak was judgment upon righteousness. "The Lord Jehovah hath sworn by his holiness, that, lo, the days [days involving judgment] shall come upon you, that they shall take you away with hooks, and your residue with fish-hooks" (4:2). For God to swear "by his holiness" means to swear by "what He is" — the Sacred, Awesome Creator and Righteous Judge of the universe. In light of "what He is" — a holy God — He must vindicate Himself and establish His holiness by punishing wickedness. Since Israel was filled with many expressions of sin, she should expect judgment in the days to come. When the judgment did come, and come it would, they would be led out through the breaches in the walls of the city, not as respected human beings but as one

53

might expect animals to be treated (4:3). They would be led out into captivity with hooks through their lips or noses as cattle being moved from one place to another. A righteous God could not tolerate an unrighteous people.

2. *The Circumstances of the Day* (4:1, 4-11). A more detailed description of the conditions within Israel-would seem to call for the necessity of the judgment of God as the prophet had warned. Look as Amos pointed to the circumstances of the day.

(1) The Place of Woman (4:1). From the time of creation woman was to have been "an help suitable." She was to have been a companion and an aid to her husband in the accomplishing of the purpose of God for their lives. Proverbs 31 gives a generous description of such a woman. Since such a noble role was the purpose of God for womankind, one would expect women of such quality in abundance in Israel. Yet this was not the case. Their role in the society of Israel (4:1) was far short of such an ideal. The wives of the nobles, the upper class, the wealthy, were characterized as being overindulgent, thoughtless, and demanding. The prophet compared them to the kine or "fat cows" of Bashan — cows produced in the fertile area of Bashan to the east of the Jordan and famous for their sleekness and fatness. The comparison suggests overindulgence, personal selfishness, and greed — all too often the characteristic of animals but never to be the characteristics of human beings, certainly not those of the women of Israel.

Yet these women had sunk to new lows in responsibility and privilege. Whereas their interest and concern should have been in the welfare of others, they were in reality only concerned for themselves. They made such demands upon their husbands — "Bring, and let us drink" — that they could not provide their demands through honest business pursuits. Their husbands were therefore driven to oppression, extortion, and violence. The victims of such oppression were inevitably the poor and the weak of the land. There is no indication that the first ladies of Samaria had ever given a passing thought to the sources of their income. They only wished to continue their feastings, revelries, and debaucheries. Their only concern was with their own desires and pleasures. Because of their unconcern for others as well as their irresponsible natures, they would fall prey to the judgment of God and would be humbled as they were led out into captivity (4:2, 3).

To neglect or ignore one's responsibility for the welfare of others and live only for self as these women had done was to endanger all held dear by them. To persist in such conduct would ultimately bring the denial of that which they most treasured. To seek to build a way of life based on injustice and to accept the resources of earth as personal possessions to be squandered upon self could but result in loss and tragedy (4: 2, 3).

(2) The Role of Religion (4:4, 5). The role of religion was in many ways as disappointing as the behavior of the women of Samaria. It was much less than might be expected of Bethel and Gilgal. Bethel was a great religious center. It was the sanctuary of the king (7:13) and was, for this reason, given a great significance among the sanctuaries. Gilgal was the place of Israel's initial encampment after crossing over the Jordan River and had probably continued as a favorite worship center through the years (I Samuel 10:8; Hosea 4:15).

Since these were two leading worship centers, Amos singled them out in his call to "come to Bethel" and "to Gilgal." He did not call them to come to worship as one might expect, but he called them to "come . . . and transgress" (4:4, 5). In doing so he was condemning their worship as unworthy and sinful. Their coming to Bethel and Gilgal provided them with nothing more nor less than an occasion "to transgress." Their worship was of no value; it was, on the other hand, a positive transgression.

God declared the religious conduct of Gilgal and Bethel to be a transgression even though it fully satisfied the mind of the worshipers. There was nothing wrong with Israel's performing the legal requirements of worship with great zeal. It was in fact right to do so. Yet in doing this, they were ignoring the inner

spiritual requirements of religion by their injustice and unconcern for the rights and needs of others. They were careful to
keep, to the letter, the requirements made for the ritual of sacrifice and the schedule of tithing. In fact, they attempted to add
to the merit of their ritual and offerings by bringing a daily
sacrifice rather than an annual one (I Samuel 1:1, 7, 21) and
by bringing their tithes every three days rather than every three
years (Deuteronomy 14:28; 26:12; Amos 4:4). They offered "a
thank-offering of leavened bread"; that is, they attempted to add
to the merit of the offering by burning a part which the laws
of sacrifice did not require to be burned. Further, the reference
to leaven — an ingredient to be withheld from offerings — probably suggests an attempt on their part to make the offering more
worthy in the belief that it would thereby be more pleasing to
God.

The reference to "publishing freewill-offerings" implies an
enthusiastic effort to establish their religious devotion by publishing their performances at worship and offerings. Such was
contrary to the entire spirit of worship. It pleased Israel (4:5),
made her feel good, helped her in thinking her faithfulness guaranteed her security and favor with God. Yet, implicitly, the
prophet suggested that it did not please God. Israel's actions
suggested that she believed that the requirement of God had
been met when the ritual of worship had been carried out.
Nothing could be further from the truth. Worship for Israel
must involve character, devotion, compassion, and concern. It
was to be more than form. Form was to have been the outer
manifestation of inner quality, or should have been at least. When
one made an offering of the heart — "a freewill-offering" — it
would be inconsistent with the act and the spirit of the offering
to cause fanfare and call attention to self. Therefore, Amos de-
nounced their worship as displeasing to God and of no real
profit to the nation (4:4, 5).

To be religious required living by the practice of the principles taught by religion, and not ritual alone. Religion was to
have form, but it was also to have an inner dedication. This

Israel lacked. Amos, therefore, declared the truth about Israel's religion. It displeased God. It was transgression, not worship. It was heartless ritualism!

(3) God's Reaction to Heartless Ritualism — the Lesson of History (4:6-11). In light of the sinful practices within the religious life of Israel, God declared that "I on my part, in return for such practices and conduct — such heartless ritualism — have done nothing but chastise" (4:6b). These chastisements should have been proof that there was no merit in ritualism alone. Ritualism alone had caused chastisement after chastisement. Amos listed a few of those which had been sent as proof of his contention.

A famine had brought hunger ("cleanness of teeth") and "want of bread" (4:6). The famine was to have been for the purpose of helping Israel see that her chastisements were the result of her heartless ritualism. Even so, she did not see it. She changed neither her attitude nor her practices. Her stubbornness kept her from turning to God and conforming to his demands for a genuine heart of devotion and service as opposed to a literalism of ritual and custom (4:6b).

The second chastisement sent as a result of a heartless ritualism took the form of a drought (4:7, 8). God had withheld the rains during the critical months of the growing season — January or February. Such would destroy the crops and render a harvest hopeless because it was the rain which fell at the beginning of the growth season that was denied. Without it there could be no crops. Even so, they did not recognize the folly of their way and turn to God.

Since neither famine nor drought had turned the nation back to God, He had sent a blight upon the crops by blasting them with the unbearable winds from the East and a form of mildew caused by a combination of heat and dampness (4:9a). Later He had sent the devastation of the locusts (4:9b) to gnaw away at any surviving crop and then the "pestilence after the manner of Egypt" (4:10). This pestilence, though not specifically stated, was most likely referred to as being a disaster as devastating as that of Egypt and may have involved the loss of the firstborn or some other such calamity.

After the calamity comparable to that of Egypt, wars had come upon the nation (4:10b). These wars may have been references to the lengthy conflict between Israel and Syria prior to Syria's overthrow by the Assyrians (II Kings 10:32, 33; 13:3, 7). Whatever the specific reference, the loss in human life had been so great and the loss of fighting animals so far-reaching that there were neither enough men nor time to clear the battlefield of the dead. The decomposing bodies had made the place of battle even more intolerable and oppressive (4:10b). Yet, all of this had not caused Israel to return to God in spirit and truth. They persisted, however, by their actions at least, that their ritual was the sole spiritual requirement

Then came the last visitation — the earthquake (4:11). It had been as destructive as the one which "overthrew Sodom and Gomorrah" (Genesis 19:24, 25); yet with one difference, some had escaped. They had been "as a brand snatched out of the burning"; that is, they had barely escaped; they had nearly gone with the rest, but by a miraculous act of Yahweh they had been delivered. Even such a miracle as that had not caused the survivors to turn to God. Nothing God had done as "an act of judgment" or as "an act of mercy," as the case may have been, had caused Israel to turn to him in genuine repentance and commitment. Therefore, in keeping with the statement of Amos 3:2, God would visit all her iniquities upon her. This situation would exceed, in degree and extent, any of those of the past, and because of it they are told to get ready for it.

3. *Preparation for Judgment* (4:12). The judgment facing Israel was not described. It was referred to as "thus." Even so, the very indefiniteness of "thus" suggests its reach and result. The future tense of the verb ("will I do") suggests a judgment yet to come upon Israel. The judgment was so certain and of such destructiveness that Israel was called to "prepare to meet thy God" (4:12b), that is, in judgment. These were not words of grace but words of judgment. These words seem to call the nation to prepare for disaster beyond any yet known. Even so,

this does not deny the possibility of individual repentance (5: 15). It does, on the other hand, seem to preclude, in this context at least, any repentance on a national scale. The nation would meet judgment of the severest kind — destruction. This destruction was not based upon God's unwillingness to forgive; it was based upon Israel's unwillingness to repent (4:6b, 8b, 10b). Such unwillingness could result in nothing but tragedy. The prophet was saying, "God is on His way in judgment; get ready for it!"

4. *The God They Will Meet* (4:13). The last statement of this chapter seems to be suggesting to any or all who may have had doubts about the ability or resources of God to follow through with His destructive judgment that He had not only the resources but also the power to bring it to pass. The God which Israel would meet in judgment was the One who made the mountains with the ease of a potter fashioning a vessel (4: 13a). He created all that the eye could see as well as that which could not be seen — "the wind" (4:13b). He was the Creator of the entire universe. Though there is no general agreement about the meaning of the next clause ("he . . . declareth unto man what is his thought"), Amos may have been referring to God's omniscience (all knowing, infinite, and universal knowledge). That is, God was the One who knew the inner secrets of man's mind and heart and was able to discern and reveal them. The next clause ("that maketh the morning darkness") may refer to the fact that God was the source of the storm which hides the light of the morning sun or that He had the ability to bring destruction of such proportion that it would blot out the morning sun. In either of these interpretations, or both, the allusions seem to be to God's great power (omnipotence) over the natural, moral, human, and material world. The last clause ("treadeth upon the high places of the earth") doubtless refers to His treading upon the clouds and/or mountains in the activity of thunder, lightning, and downpour. Such would suggest His presence in many or all places at one time, that is, His omnipresence. He was in their midst but was also active in the heavens.

The description of God given here was a description of the

God of Israel – known as "Yahweh, the God of hosts" (4:13).
The God of Israel was the Creator, the all-knowing, the all-
powerful, and the all-present God. Since He was who He was
and what He was, Israel must not doubt that He was able to
perform whatever He willed for the nation. If He willed destruction, He had the resources to bring it to pass. He would
not be inconsistent with Himself or His purpose in doing so.
Therefore, since judgment had been announced, Israel must get
ready for the onslaught. It was an evil time; the signs everywhere revealed it. God, being what He is, would do something
about it; judgment was coming. Israel could only get ready for
it. It would seem that she had reached the point of no return.
The "signs of the times" seem to have borne out that truth.

FOR FURTHER STUDY

1. Read the articles on "Bashan" in ZPBD and IDB, I, 363-364.
2. Read the discussion of "Gilgal" in *Ancient Israel* by R. de
   Vaux, pp. 302-303.
3. For a discussion of "blasting" see the article on "Blight" in
   IDB, I, 448 or in some other Bible Dictionary.
4. For a discussion of "mildew" see the article in IDB, III, 378.
5. For a discussion on the "palmer-worm" see the article on
   "Locust" in IDB, III, 144-148.
6. Read the article on "Sacrifices" in *Ancient Israel* by R. de
   Vaux, pp. 415-423.
7. Discuss the role of woman in society. Is there a relationship
   between the ethics and morality of woman and that of the
   nation? Discuss.
8. Is it possible for a person or nation to sin at worship? Is this
   what Israel did as she went to Bethel and Gilgal? What
   current conditions, if any, may be compared with those in
   Israel and Judah?
9. List those conditions in history which have been interpreted
   as chastisements of God. What effect did they have? What
   effect should they have had?

CHAPTER 6

WHEN RELIGION FAILS
(Amos 5:1-27)

Nothing is so important to the life of an individual or a nation as the character of its religion. The future of a nation is vitally related to the worship of its people. To worship the true God in the wrong way or to compromise and worship other gods along with, or in addition to, Yahweh could but result in disfavor with God and judgment from God. To establish these truths, Amos returned to amplify what he had already pointed out in 4:4, 5.

1. *The Lamentation over Israel* (5:1-3). This discourse, which deals primarily with the heartless and meaningless formalism of Israel's religion, begins with a lamentation over the house of Israel. Though lamentations or dirges, as they are most frequently called, were generally voiced as the result of a great calamity to express the grief of those affected by the disaster, Amos sang one over Israel *before* the tragedy befell her. He evidently did so because he believed the conditions within the nation were so destructive that the punishment of God was as good as realized. He sang as though Israel had already fallen (5:2a). Doubtless this method was for effect,

and it must have been a sobering thing for those assembled to listen to the prophet as he sang their own funeral song.

Following the dirge, the prophet described the conditions within Israel which called forth the wrath along with the one possibility which they had for hope.

2. *The Way of Israel* (5:5). The religious conduct of Israel is best characterized by heartless ritualism. The religious activity of the nation was associated with the ancient worship centers of Bethel, Gilgal, and Beersheba. It was most probable, in light of the pronounced judgment upon two of the three places mentioned, that these "worship centers" had corrupted every expression of true and sincere worship. To worship at these centers, and likely others not mentioned, was to participate in a false, heartless, meaningless ritualism which resulted in spiritual blindness and social injustice. Such practices could but result in tragedy. This Amos revealed in the contrast drawn between the true and sincere worship of God suggested in the words "seek ye me, and ye shall find life" and the predicted destruction of Gilgal and Bethel as well as those who visit them (5:5b). Gilgal would be devastated, and Bethel (house of God) would become Beth-aven (house of nought). Beersheba, though not included with Bethel and Gilgal in the statement of judgment, was by implication as subject to judgment as the others because it was listed on their side of the ledger. Thus, their very consignment to judgment established the unworthiness of these centers and the falsity of the worship being carried on there.

The way of Israel was, then, the way of heartless ritualism. Their flooding the worship centers meant nothing of spiritual value and ethical consequence. They had, in fact, been spiritually blinded by the ritual conducted there. For had their worship been genuine, it would have made a difference in their daily conduct.

3. *The Result of Heartless Ritualism in Conduct* (5:7, 10). Genuine worship ultimately expresses itself in the conduct of the worshiper. So does sheer ritualistic worship. The conduct of Israel decried any sincerity or integrity in their worship. They had turned the sweetness of justice into wormwood and

"cast down righteousness to the earth" (5:7). The leaders and
their nobles, whenever they had occasion, would so engage in
injustice that bitterness would be the portion of those falling
into their hands. Wormwood is a plant producing a bitter nox-
ious juice (Deuteronomy 29:18; Proverbs 5:4) and was cited
here for the purpose of characterizing an event which created
an excessively bitter experience for the ones involved in it. Thus
the prophet charged Israel with displacing the sweetness of
justice with the wormwood (bitterness) of injustice.

The second effect of Israel's ritualism was that they "cast
down righteousness to the earth" (5:7b). Righteousness was
the practice of justice and right in any and every realm. In
this context it referred particularly to civil justice. Those in
authority, with responsibility, were charged with "casting down
righteousness" as though it were a person and then trampling
it under foot through their exaltation of injustice and oppressive
practices in their dealings with the poor and weak of society.

Finally, those who failed to worship in truth turned in hate
upon "him that reproveth in the gate, and they abhorred him
that spoke uprightly" (5:10). The ones administering justice
in the gate (the place where the judges sat and held court)
hated (detested) the prophet or judge who called them to task
for their unjust decisions. They abhorred (a stronger term than
hate) those who took up the cause of those being unjustly treated
as though such did not deserve the privilege of an advocate. In
other words, those dealing in injustice despised those who called
for a quality of character befitting men so zealous in the practice of their ritual. Yet this was their greatest problem; their
ritual was heartless and formal and thereby of ill effect rather
than good.

4. *The Effect of Heartless Ritualism upon the Prudent*
(5:13). The prudent, who understood the basis of justice and
who had readily seen through its abuse in Israel, realized the
possible dangers and probable futility of changing the existing
conditions and therefore remained silent. Though Amos did not
give his approval to their silence, he did state the conditions as
they existed in Israel. Even though there were those who re-

mained silent, Amos himself refused to accept such a role and persisted in pointing to the conditions (2:6-8; 7:15) as they really were. Surely he must have expected no less of the others. Yet, they remained silent and by their very silence encouraged the continuation of injustice and oppression which had become so widespread.

5. *The Effect of Heartless Ritualism upon God* (5:21-23). Israel surely must have thought that her religious activism and enthusiasm would delight God and insure His continuous favor. It must have been a most disconcerting thing to hear the prophet describe their ritual as abominable to God when he declared that God was not only unsympathetic but that He was openly hostile to their religious practices. Amos did this in his announcement that God "hates," yes, "despises" their feasts and solemn assemblies (5:21). The key word in the verse is "your." It was *their own* feasts and gatherings, which did not really represent Yahweh, that created such an attitude on God's part. Yahweh would not take any delight in their solemn assemblies (5:21). They had been conceived by Israel, not by God, and initiated through ulterior motives (4:22, 23) rather than through genuine spiritual concern.

Amos then enumerated those feasts despised and rejected by Yahweh (5:22). First, God would not accept their burnt-offerings (Leviticus 1) — offerings which symbolized the total commitment of the offerer to God — because there was gross inconsistency between the offering and their personal commitment. Second, He would not accept their meat-offerings (Leviticus 2) — offerings which acknowledged God as the source of the fruits of one's labor — because He could not in anywise be identified with such injustice and oppression. Last, God would not accept their peace-offerings (Leviticus 3)—offerings at which God condescended to become Israel's guest and to allow the offerer the fellowship of His presence — because there could be no fellowship with those who treated their brothers unjustly. All of these offerings were unacceptable because the religion of the Israelites was nothing but heartless ritual. Their conduct gave them away. Had their worship been genuine, their private and collective conduct would have been different. A proper relationship with God would have established a right relationship among men.

After declaring the rejection of their feasts, Amos added God's displeasure with their singing and music (5:23). In doing so, it is doubtful that He was singling out their music for special condemnation but simply noting another aspect of their entire worship procedure. God was displeased with every aspect of their worship! Genuineness was lacking; formalism and heartless ritualism were widespread. Their worship was, in its every expression, a thing which displeased God.

6. *The Result of God's Attitude* (5:27). Because of the inconsistency between the worship and conduct of Israel, the nation would be sent into captivity (5:27). There would be such suffering and devastation that every street would be filled with those bewailing and bemoaning the disaster (5:16). Not even the vineyards — usually associated with joy and happiness — were to escape the passing through of Yahweh (5:17). This time there was to be no Passover for Israel as at the time of the Exodus (Exodus 12:13). This time He would pass through the nation as He did through Egypt long ago (Exodus 12:12). Such a mission by God in judgment will so prostrate Israel (5:2a) that all her own resources as well as those of all her allies would not be able to render her the necessary assistance to stand again (5:2b). Her armies would be so reduced that there would remain but a handful (5:3). Any hope or promise she may have had would be gone.

Even the hope which the nation may have had in the Day of the Lord would prove disappointing (5:18). That "day" which was to have ushered in the nation's great era of glory would never be realized by those who worshiped through a heartless ritualism and lived by injustice. That "day," when it came, would set justice and righteousness in their rightful places. Israel, lacking both, would find it a "day" without hope. It would be, contrary to every expectation, a day of darkness rather than light (5:18b). The darkness of the "day" suggests the loss of every avenue of escape. Israel would be like the men who sought to "flee from a lion, and a bear met him, or went into the house and leaned his hand on the wall, and a serpent bit him" (5:19). Every avenue of escape would be closed to those who on account of pretense in religion sinned against God and their fellow man. "To hope for justification in the day of the Lord," said Amos, "would but result in utter disappointment and darkness." The day of the Lord for Israel would be a day of judgment — "pitch darkness" — and not a day of deliverance. It would be thus because Israel had not sought Jehovah with her heart, that she might live.

7. *Israel's One Avenue of Hope* (5:4, 6, 14, 15). Despite the grim prospects of the imminent fall of Israel, as it would be experienced in the Exile, chapter 5 is interspersed with references of hope. The first of these (5:4 and also 5:6) was an admonition to "seek (turn to) the Lord," that is, to turn to God in true devotion and obedience to his law and purpose. To serve and worship God certainly involved sacrifices but not sacrifice alone; it involved a right relationship with God which would result in right conduct. Yet where sacrifices were involved, these were to be conducted according to Mosaic legislation. They were not to be changed nor added to, as was often the case in Israel. The sacrifices of the Chosen People were to be as they had been in the wilderness — in simplicity and devotion. Since Israel had not been required to participate in elaborate ritual in the wilderness, a period generally idealized as one of remarkable closeness between God and Israel, it was not required now (5:25). In fact, the ritual which they now practiced in zeal and elaborateness was positively harmful. It was heartless and formal. It blinded them to true spirituality.

The nation was further admonished to "seek good, and not evil, that ye may live; and so Jehovah, the God of hosts, will be with you, as ye say" (5:14). The words "seek good" are about the same as "seek Jehovah" (5:4, 6). Those committed to doing good and not evil, as Israel had been in afflicting "the just, taking bribes, and turning aside the needy in the gate from their right" (5:12), would find that Jehovah would be with them to give continued existence and blessing. To "seek good" would not only bring blessing, but it would also require the seeker "to hate evil" (5:15), and "to hate evil" would require "seeking good." The standard for determining the good and evil was not a human standard but was based upon the manifest will of God (5:24).

When men sought to do God's will, then justice would roll down into the practices of society as a continuous stream, and righteousness would enter into life's relationships at an unremitting pace (5:24). To "seek Jehovah" in truth would mean opening the gates of justice and righteousness that they might flow uninterruptedly into every realm of the nation's life. Such a condition within Israel would secure her continued existence. It was the will of God for Israel. Less than this would result in disaster.

8. *The Alternative to Turning Godward* (5:6, 26, 27). That all might know the consequences of not turning to God, the prophet declared that God was going to send them "into captivity beyond Damascus" (5:27). When this judgment did come upon Israel, ninety per cent of her population would lose their lives (5:3). A devouring fire woud break out in the house of Joseph (Israel), and there was no one in Bethel to put it out (5:6). This was because God was not there. He was opposed to Bethel. It was an abominable place to God because it had kept Israel from turning to Him in genuine repentance. The alternative to turning to God in repentance — which meant life — was disobedience and captivity. Israel, having chosen disobedience, thereby chose captivity. When the judgment fell, they would "take up" (to bear into exile) Sakkut, their king, and Kaiwan, their star god — both being Assyrian gods — and go into captivity with them as well as on account of them (5:26, RSV).

Thus, Amos has given a vivid and tragic picture of a nation whose religion had failed. It had failed because it had become a heartless ritualism. This kind of religion had allowed formalism and idolatry to enter their worship and injustice and oppression to enter their human relationships. Their religion had therein been a failure. It had brought death rather than life and darkness rather than light. Even the chosen nation could not expect to escape the consequences predetermined by spiritual blindness brought into existence by heartless and meaningless formalism. Since this was true, neither could any other nation expect to escape.

The fruit of heartless ritualism in any age of religious practice will be death and darkness. The need of every generation is a genuine and sincere relationship to God in repentance and faith. This will not only transform the person; it will also reform the society. Both of these were needed in ancient Israel. They are needed now.

FOR FURTHER STUDY

1. Read the article on "Wormwood" in the IDB, IV, 878-879.
2. Read the articles on "Pleiades" in IDB, III, 826 and on "Orion" in IDB, III, 609 or some other Bible Dictionary.
3. What is to be the true relationship between religion and ethics or morality? What was the relationship in the life of Israel? Is there a vital relationship in modern society? If not, why? If so, how?
4. What is the attitude of modern society toward the prophet or those who speak soberly about existing conditions?
5. What was Israel's hope in the Day of Yahweh? Do you think they were disillusioned when the prophet spoke as he did in 5:18-20? What does the Day of Yahweh mean to the present generation? Why? Discuss.
6. What was the basis of God's dissatisfaction with Israel's worship? Does God hate? Is the worship of the modern church pleasing to God? If so, why? If not, what can be done to make it more pleasing? Discuss.

CHAPTER 7

THE TRAGEDY OF WASTED OPPORTUNITY
(Amos 6)

No other nation in human history had such opportunity to bless all mankind as did Israel. Her history was filled with many remarkable providences. God chose her, provided for her needs and guaranteed her future, but only in order that she might be an avenue of blessing to others (Genesis 12:1-3). When the nation failed to measure up to its opportunities, its true religious leaders called them to task and warned them of the consequences. It was now time for such a warning again. Amos sought to deliver that warning in the chapter before us. He did so by revealing Israel's attitude toward those God-given resources which had been entrusted to her.

1. *The Resources of Israel* (6:1, 2). The first resources alluded to by the prophet were religious and military. In pronouncing woe upon those "at ease in Zion and secure in the mountain of Samaria" (6:1), the prophet was coming to grips with the false sense of security (ease) held by those in Samaria as well as in Zion back in his own country where the same condition existed. Together they were interpreting the religious advantage of being a people with whom God dwelled as well as their military resources as guarantees of an indestructible security. Both of these were advantages which had accrued from

their relationship to Yahweh. Their spiritual and military strength both came from God. He was the One who dwelt in her midst and had led her hosts (armies) to victory. The presence of God in the midst of His people as well as His leadership in battle were unique resources. No other nations had known such advantages as the Covenant People.

Turning from its religious and military resources, Amos next noted the human resources of the nation — "the notable men of the chief of the nations, to whom the house of Israel came!" (6:1b). These human resources belonged to "the chief of the nations" — chief by virtue of their relationship to God and the world (Genesis 12:1-3; Exodus 19:5). Belonging to "the chief of the nations" of the earth suggests that they were resourceful men, enlightened men — men of worth and accomplishment (6:1b). They were leaders and judges to whom the people came in search of justice (II Samuel 15:4) and who rendered special service to the nation. These men, known by God, knew God and His law. In such men Israel realized a resource (a human resource) beyond that enjoyed by the other nations. The men of the other nations may have been resourceful and wise indeed, but the men of Israel had privileges beyond theirs. They were known of God, and they knew God.

More recent interpreters of Amos suggest that the prophet's reference to "the notable men of the chief of the nations" is irony. They suggest that this was their own opinion of themselves. It may well be irony, and it may reflect their opinion of themselves, but it would also seem to reflect a truth which was generally acknowledged in the Biblical attitude toward Israel. Israel was chief among the nations in so far as the purpose of God for her was concerned. She was to have been the avenue of blessing to all other nations. This was a unique role which no other peoples had.

Lastly, the prophet, turning to a specific comparison of Israel with other kingdoms, suggested that none could compare with Israel in their material resources (6:2). There is every reason to believe that the material wealth of Irsael did exceed that of the surrounding kingdoms at this time in her history. Therefore, this statement of comparison followed.

If the interpretation of this section be valid, and it must be stated that there is no general agreement, then Amos had placed his finger upon one of the most vulnerable areas in Israel's life: her use of the resources entrusted to her by God.

The unique relationship between Israel and God (compare 3:2a) was the basis of her acquisition of these resources. The Old Testament writers were willing to acknowledge this, and they saw Israel placed under grave responsibility because of God's relationship to and provision for her. For them, and now Amos in particular, the nation's response to her responsibility, her use of her resources, would determine her future.

2. *Israel's Use of Her Resources* (6:1, 4-6, 12). The conditions known to exist in Israel at this time and the message of Amos make it quite plain that Israel had misspent and misused the resources placed at her disposal.

First, Judah and doubtless Israel also interpreted the spiritual resources, which came from God's presence, as an absolute security. They were God's people; He dwelt in their midst; they had nothing to fear. No harm could befall them no matter the conditions within the nation. Yet the pronouncement of "woe" (6:1) by Amos indicates that they had not properly interpreted the resources accruing from God's presence, nor had they used them to better the conditions of the poor and oppressed by practicing the righteousness revealed by the One dwelling in their midst. It also suggests that they had improperly interpreted their military resources. The mere possession of military resources did not mean that they were invincible. Their security rested upon more than military might. It ultimately rested upon their relationship to God and His purpose. Their security rested upon what they were and upon what they did with that which God had furnished them, not upon what they had.

Turning to the use of their human resources, Amos declared that they had used their insight, knowledge, and understanding (their human resources) to further their own selfish designs and ends. They had "turned justice into gall, and the fruit of righteousness into wormwood" (6:12). That is, these "notable men of the chief nations" had allowed themselves to be used by the nation or had used their place of leadership and authority in the nation to serve their own purposes. Those able to afford the price of their favor in defiance of the knowledge and understanding which they supposedly had or which they should have had as "chief men" would have every advantage. Those unable to buy their favor were at the greatest disadvantage. Thus, Israel had tragically wasted her human resources. These "chief men" had not served the lofty purposes of justice and righteousness as God had instructed or as He had intended. Those who were to have been a source of blessing to all men everywhere, became in reality sources of pain and harm. The nation had misused one of its greatest resources — its "chief men" who were to have established justice in the land.

Finally, Amos turned to the use which they had made of their material possessions. They had squandered their plenty upon themselves in selfish indulgence (6:4-6). They lay upon beds with expensive ivory inlay in the shade of their awnings and ate the choice lambs of the flock (ate "the lambs out of the flock") and their specially fattened "calves out of the midst of the stall" without the slightest show of concern for the needs of others. They sang "idle songs to the sound of the viol," invented "for themselves instruments of music, like David," drank "wine in bowls," and anointed "themselves with the chief oils." The picture was that of a nation in which the wealthy were totally consumed with themselves and their own selfish pleasure. They were so concerned with themselves that they forgot about the needs and the desires of others. They wrongly interpreted their material prosperity as an evidence of God's pleasure with them and as a reward for their faithfulness. They should have interpreted it as a blessing to be shared with the poor and the needy. Instead they took the resources made available to them by the providence of God for the good of all men and cut them short by squandering them upon their own little selfish lives! Such practices were filled with folly and unspeakable danger. The very justice of God attaches danger to such a selfish way of life.

3. *The Danger of Israel's Folly* (6:6b,3a). The folly of Israel's way may be seen in two things. First, their conduct and their attitude toward others had caused them to put "far away the evil day" (6:3a). Their encouragement of the oppression of the poor and the less fortunate (6:3b), a thing which they profited in and thereby delighted in, had caused them (in mind at least) to declare distant the day of judgment upon evil. They acted as though "that day" were too remote to have any vital effect upon them. Their one concern was their own self-satisfaction and pleasure. This had blinded them to the reality of judgment. They had blotted it out of their minds. They did not have or would not take time to think of it. Things were going so well for them that nothing could alter their condition in the future. Therefore, why think about such "a day"? It was too remote to even be considered!

The second factor indicating Israel's folly was the utter unconcern and indifference to the wounds which the conduct of the leaders had already brought upon the nation and the wounds which would yet be brought upon it because of their injustice and oppression (6:6b). The reference was to the present and the future. The present wound had reference to the hurt inflicted by the abundance of the rich and the poverty of poor caused by the injustice of their leaders and the oppression of the needy. The future hurt was a greater hurt which would come upon the nation because of the hurt which had already come into it. It was as though the present hurt had already entered the larger hurt and had determined ultimate ruin for the nation (6:7a).

4. *The Unreasonableness of Israel's Practices* (6:12). In seeking to awaken Israel to her folly, Amos turnd to the unreasonableness of the things going on within the nation. He turned to natural law in an attempt to help them see what they had done. He began his effort with the question, "Shall horses run upon the rock?" (6:12a). It was a question which dealt with the reasonableness of horses running upon the cliffs where

wild goats usually roam — cliffs high, precipitous, covered with shale, and associated with danger and death. The answer implied in the question would be "no!" It would be an unreasonable thing, even a disastrous thing to run horses there, since the horse and rider, if the animal were mounted, would surely be destroyed as a result of slipping and the inevitable fall upon the rocks below. It was as though the prophet were saying, "There is no greater unreasonableness to be found than that of running a horse upon the rocks of a cliff. Anyone of reason would know better — no man of knowledge would run such a risk."

The second question asked was "will one plow there with oxen?" (6:12b) or, as most translate it, "does one plow the sea with oxen?" This question, like the first, suggests an unreasonable practice and implies an emphatic "no!" Whichever form of the question one may choose, whether plowing the cliffs or the sea, the point is the same: either labor is unreasonable and to no avail. Neither cliff nor sea would produce anything but disappointment and heartache for the tiller. Therefore, the effort would be an unreasonable one. It was a thing a knowledgeable, reasonable man would never attempt. This was the point of both questions. They were suggesting the unreasonableness, danger, even destructiveness associated with defying the natural laws of the universe, or better, the laws of prudence. A wise man, a knowledgeable man would never resort to running horses on cliffs or plowing in the sea with oxen. Israel with all her understanding would never engage in pursuits so fraught with danger and so identified with unprofitableness. She knew better than to defy the laws of nature. Her understanding of nature and her laws would keep her from it.

Though Israel knew better than to defy the laws of nature, Amos declared that she had defied the laws (rule) of God — laws requiring compassion and justice in all human relationships. This she had done in turning "justice into gall and the fruit of righteousness into wormwood" (6:12b) and causing "the seat of violence to come near" (6:3b); that is, she had defied the moral laws of God by administering them in such a way as to cause bitterness and hurt instead of sweetness and helpfulness.

Israel had also defied the rule (law) of God by boasting that she had become what she was by her own strength. Her boast involved the conquest of Lo-debar and Karnaim, small cities of the kingdom of Damascus located on the east side of the Jordan River (6:13, rsv). Lo-debar means "a thing of nought," and Karnaim means "horns" or "power." In having boasted of her military successes over these towns, Israel had ignored the role which Jehovah had played in them. They had in their boasting failed to acknowledge the help of God. Therefore, the prophet held their victory up to scorn by referring to the one town which meant "a thing of nought" and the other which meant "horns, symbols of power," as though they were of such little significance that to have boasted of these victories was vain. He seemed to suggest that the thing which Israel had boasted of having done on her own was of such insignificance that it was unworthy even of mentioning, let alone boasting.

5. *The Result of Israel's Unreasonableness and Folly* (6:7-11, 14). Amos turned now to make known the consequences of Israel's unreasonable attitudes and practices. They would go into captivity. This was revealed in the words: "For, behold, I will raise up against you a nation, O house of Israel . . . ; and they shall afflict you from the entrance of Hamath unto the brook of Arabah" (6:14). Here God declared that he would cause Israel to be oppressed (crushed) from one end of the country, "the entrance of Hamath," to the other, "the brook of Arabah." This oppression would have a disastrous effect. There would be a deportation (captivity), and the first in line to go would be those who had been leading Israel in her folly (6:7). That which they had acquired through their oppression and injustice would be destroyed (6:8b).

Samaria, the capital city, would receive the brunt of the blow. Its men and wealth (goods and animals) would be given over to the conquerors. The loss in life as a result of the invasion would be staggering. Those who survived the war would die from a plague (6:9). Entire families would be wiped out.

The accumulation of the dead would be of such proportion, or their corpses would be so disease laden that the bodies would have to be burned rather than buried. When a survivor was found and inquired of by those performing the last rites, he would advise silence out of fear that in their conversation Yahweh's name might be invoked and because of such an invocation, further destruction would fall upon them (6:10).

Thus Amos revealed that Israel's poor stewardship of responsibility and her squandering of the resources furnished her by God could but end in destruction and death. Such injustice and unconcern required judgment. They need expect nothing less. It was tragic that such an opportunity to bless men should have been squandered by Israel through her abuse and misuse of the resources given her by the providence of God. She knew better, yet she refused to do better. Disaster was the result of her refusal.

How great the tragedy of wasted opportunity!

FOR FURTHER STUDY

1. Read articles on "Calneh," I, 490; "Hamath," II, 516; and "Gath," II, 355ff., in IDB or ZPBD.
2. List those practices in Israel which distracted her and kept her from considering seriously the potential judgment which could come upon her.
3. Are any of these practices found within society today? Which ones?
4. Was Israel concerned with the harm done herself through injustice and unrighteousness? Why not?
5. What judgment was announced upon Israel for her sins? What disaster befell the nation in 722 B.C.? What relationship does the Bible suggest between that disaster and the character of the nation?
6. Does God still judge nations? List those you believe to be examples. Why were those special ones chosen?

CHAPTER 8

GOD, THE PROPHET, AND THE WORLD
(Amos 7)

1. The Visions and God (7:1-9)
2. The World's Reaction to the Prophet (7:10-13)
3. The Witness of the Prophet (7:14-17)

Chapter 7 contains three of the prophet's visions, each with its own particular emphasis and purpose. Together they teach a great deal about the nature of Israel's God and His method of dealing with the nation. This section also contains the personal experience of the prophet, as he was chosen, and the reaction of the nation to a ministry of the kind given Amos.

1. *The Visions and God* (7:1-9). The first vision was that of the locust plague. It may have been initiated by an actual appearance of locusts. As Amos stood meditating on the potential destructiveness of the locusts which had appeared, God took control of his mind and revealed to him a deeper truth — he "saw" in the locust plague a parable of what was in store for the nation Israel. His insight was the work of God. "He caused the prophet to see" what Israel faced on account of sin. He through the vision conceived that God was about to fall upon Israel in as destructive a way as the locusts would upon the defenseless crop. They could no more expect to survive the judgment of God than they could expect the crop to survive the locusts.

The time of the locust plague was "in the beginning of the shooting up of the latter growth" (7:1). This was the time of the second crop. It was the harvest which supplied the needs of the population after the king's due had been paid with the first ingathering. That the plague should come at this time, before the individual could harvest for his own need, would be more tragic than otherwise because of the great numbers of citizens who would suffer as a result of the loss of food which would have, apart from the locusts, met their needs.

Realizing the desperate plight in store for those in the vision should such a calamity come, the prophet besought the Lord on their behalf (7:2). Yahweh heard the prophet, and out of sorrow and sympathy for the nation, decreed that the plague of locusts should not be. In doing so, he revealed his willingness to be merciful and forgiving. Certainly this was the message Amos sought to convey to the nation. It was as though he were saying, "God is merciful; turn to Him in repentance; and He will deliver you from destruction!"

In this vision, as well as the one to follow, the prophet appears in the role of intercessor. Though his primary role was to have been that of a spokesman for God to His people, it must not be overlooked that at times the prophet became a spokesman for the people to God. This was not an innovation in the function of the prophet. Amos was following in the best tradition because both Moses (for example, Exodus 32:11-14, 30-32; Numbers 14:13-19) and Samuel (for example, I Samuel 7:8 f.; 12:19-23), his prophetic predecssors, had interceded for the Israelites on former occasions. Amos was following in a noble tradition and even though the incident was in a vision, it revealed a great deal not only about the nature of Yahweh and His disposition to forgive Israel but also the responsibility of the prophet for those to whom he prophesied. He was not only a messenger with a message from God, but also an intercessor on their behalf.

The second vision (7:4-6) was that of a devastating drought. It may have been suggested to the prophet as he looked upon a fire which raged across the parched earth destroying everything in its path or as he witnessed the withering heat of the sun as it consumed the vegetation. In either case, as he stood watching, God caused the prophet to "see" that something equally as devastating lay in store for the sinful nation. Israel was about to fall into the hands of an oppressor who would be as destructive as the sun or the fire. Note that it was no ordinary conflagration. It was of such intensity that it not only threatened the land itself but also the "deep" beneath; that is, it would, if it broke forth, destroy all of the earth which was visible, as well as the sub-terrestrial which could not be seen.

Once again, after the petition of the prophet, God repented concerning (felt sorry for) the judgment decreed and willed a change. In willing a change He declared, "This also shall not be" (7:6). Even though Israel's sin was great, Yahweh stood ready to forgive her wickedness if she would turn from her evil in sincere repentance. The petition on the part of the prophet and the resultant deliverance by God would seem to prove that this was the message He sought to convey. Even so, there was no indication that repentance on Israel's part would be forthcoming; therefore, Amos received a third vision in which there was no intercession on the part of the prophet nor any expression of remission on God's part.

The third vision (7:7-9) may have been suggested as the prophet stood watching a man working to plumb a wall which no longer stood erect. As Amos stood there, the Lord "showed," not locusts, or fire, but himself standing "upon (beside) a wall erected by a plumbline, with a plumbline in his hand" (7:7). As the prophet beheld this sight, a voice inquired as to what he saw, and he responded, "A plumbline." "Then said the Lord, Behold, I will set a plumbline in the midst of my people Israel, I will not again pass by them any more" (7:8). In making the statement God was revealing that He was about to test Israel by the standard used to build the wall (the very structure of the nation itself).

It was the standard of mutual trust, dependence, and faithfulness (compare Exodus 20:22 - 23:33). They were to be His people, and He would be their God. Even so, Israel had leaned away from the standard and would now be judged by it. She did not measure up; her idolatry, injustice, and unrighteousness threw her out of plumb. Therefore, judgment would come upon her. Israel would not again experience a Passover (7:8b) as they had in Egypt; that is, when God came in judgment this time, they would not be passed over as they had been in Egypt. They had reached the point of no return (compare Jeremiah 7: 16; 11:14; 14:11; 15:1), not because God would not have received them had they genuinely sought Him but because they would not turn to Him in sincere repentance.

Consequently, the "house of Jeroboam" and all Israel's sanctuaries (buildings) would be destroyed by a devastation wrought by the Lord Himself (7:9). The instrument He would use would be a nation which would destroy and lead into captivity (7:17).

In the three visions already discussed, as well as the ones to be considered subsequently, God was revealing through the inner mind of the prophet imminent possibilities as a result of sin. As Amos shared his visions, he attempted to help Israel see the kind of God she served as well as the dangers of betraying Him. He was a God who persistently revealed His will and purpose. His will was not concealed but manifest. This is seen in the words, "Thus the Lord Jehovah showed me" (7:1a). He was, also, a God of judgment (7:1b, 4b) as well as a personal God who cared for those facing judgment (7:3). In addition, He was a God with a standard by which judgment was determined, as seen in the vision of the plumb-line (7:8).

Therefore, because of Yahweh's nature, it was expedient for Israel to give serious thought to her relationship to Him and to the sin within her life which had brought that relationship to the breaking point. Yet she refused. She refused to see herself as she really was and showed her attitude by seeking to silence Amos. This refusal is best seen in the spirit of Amaziah, who represented the attitude and thinking of the majority of Israel's responsible citizens.

2. *The World's Reaction to the Prophet* (7:10-13). There has always been a first time for everything. The ministry of Amos was no exception. He provided Amaziah and Jeroboam with a first. No prophet had ever stood at the king's sanctuary and declared the judgment of God as forthrightly as had this man from Judah. Yet, Amos, undoubtedly aware of the possible consequences, did not seem to show the slightest hesitancy. He

stood at the royal sanctuary to declare death to those who had permitted, even encouraged, the injustices which were everywhere in the land. He declared that their evil would bring captivity to the whole nation (7:11). These were hard words and unwelcome words. In reporting them, Amaziah said, "The kingdom could not bear all his words" (7:10). Such words had the potential for creating chaos and possible revolution.

As Amaziah repeated the words of Amos to Jeroboam, he may have been seeking to impress the king with the fact that if Israel took this man seriously, there might be an uprising on the part of the nation, an uprising demanding justice and righteousness, which could lead to a new social and religious awakening. If so, such would prove costly to Jeroboam, who was king; to Amaziah, the religious leader of a decadent formalism; as well as the other princes and leaders.

On the other hand, Amaziah may have been saying, "If what he says is true, we cannot expect to survive. We are wiped out. There is no escape. The nation cannot hope to survive." In either case, and the former may be the better explanation, based on their attempt to silence Amos, his words were unwelcomed. Therefore, Amaziah sought to turn him back to his own homeland (7:12), where he would no longer provide a threat and where he could make a livelihood (eat bread) by prophesying (compare Micah 3:5; I Kings 22:13). The very fact that he did this shows that he saw Amos as another of those who prophesied for what they could get out of their prophesying or as one who prophesied only when it proved to be personally advantageous. Amos would not allow himself to be thought of in this manner. He would challenge Amaziah's implied suggestion.

3. *The Witness of the Prophet* (7:14-17). As Amos faced what was perhaps the greatest challenge in his whole life, he began by stating his credentials. He first wished to refute the suggestion that he was just another prophet who made pronouncements and declarations which were personally advantageous. Thus he denied being a member of the popular prophetic guild or a prophet who had inherited his office, as the case may have been. Instead, he declared himself to be a prophet who

had been laid hold of by God, and he announced that "Yahweh took me from following the flock, and Yahweh said unto me, Go, prophesy unto my people Israel" (7:15). That which he had done he had done under constraint. Since his call was from God, he could do nothing but His bidding. He could not change his course nor alter his message. God had called him and given him a message; he had no alternative nor intention of doing anything other than that which God had commissioned him to do (compare 3:8).

In that frame of reference, Amos returned to his "old theme," as unpopular and unwelcome as it had been, and pressed on with his proclamation of judgment (7:17). Neither threat, intimidation, nor hostility could silence a man with his credentials. The unwillingness of men to accept the truth of what he had said did not discourage him nor turn him back from his mission. He insisted that Israel would "be led away captive out of his land" (7:17c). Disbelief and/or hostility would have nothing to do with his persistence in proclaiming the judgment as may be seen as he turned to deal more pointedly with the judgment which would fall upon Amaziah himself. Fully aware of what he was doing, he prophesied tragedy for Amaziah's family and their possessions as well as death for Amaziah in a foreign land ("a land that is unclean" [7:17]).

Through all his forthright dealings with the priesthood and the crown, Amos remained dauntless and courageous. He, unafraid, aware of the dangers involved, kept at his task — a task which he might not have enjoyed, but one which he nevertheless believed to be God-given and which he could not and would not refrain from doing (3:8). This was as it should always be when the man of God faces an unfriendly world. He must take the message wheresoever and to whomsoever he may be directed to go. The true prophet must face his opposition with courage and conviction. He must be willing to pay any price at any time to realize God's purpose for his life and work. Amos stood willing and ready for any and every eventuality.

FOR FURTHER STUDY

1. What did Amos mean when he said, "The Lord Jehovah showed me . . ."? Does God still show men? Discuss.
2. Did Amaziah represent the "religious establishment" of his day? Do you think there was anything selfish about what he did? What? Discuss.
3. Make a list of several persons you believe to have been called. What evidences have you found to suggest their having been so? Are any of the attitudes and declarations found in the call of Amos to be found in those listed? Which ones? What do these suggest?
4. Is the courage of Amos a virtue worthy of emulation? Would such a display be accepted by you or your city? If not, why? If so, how would you explain it?

CHAPTER 9

WHEN SIN RIPENS
(Amos 8)

1. The Hampering of Summer Fruit (8:1, 2)
2. A Contrast in Harvest Time (8:3)
3. The Fruit Israel Bore (8:4-6)
4. The Result of a Crop of Sin (8:7-14)
5. The Gatherer of Israel's Crop (8:2b)

In continuing with the visions, Amos recounted the revelation received in the vision of the summer fruit. Summer fruit was that fruit identified with the completion of the harvest season. The vision suggested to the mind of the prophet that just as the summer fruit indicated the final ingathering of the season, so would there be a final harvest of sin from which the nation would "never rise up again." The end for Israel was fast drawing near. The years of Israel's promise and grace had nearly run out; her place of privilege was all but gone. God was about to gather the last crop Israel would produce.

1. *The Hampering of Summer Fruit* (8:1, 2). The vision of summer fruit may have come to the prophet as he stood gazing upon a basket laden with the last fruit of the season. The significance of the summer fruit was in the fact that it was the last of the season to be gathered. The Hebrew word for summer fruit sounds very much like the word for *end*, so the prophet, by a play on words, was announcing a solemn truth. That truth was that as there was a final harvest for each season, so there was a final harvest for sin.

The Lord used the truth of the last harvest to reveal to the prophet that Israel's season for turning to him had come

to its conclusions (8:2). The last harvest season was upon them.
All of Israel's past seemed to be converging at one point. The
crop which she had planted — a crop of idolatry, unrighteousness, and injustice — was about to be gathered. It would be the
severest sort of harvest. It would not only be the last harvest
of the season, but there was a sense in which it would also be
the last season (8:14c). The whole tone of the vision was dark
and somber. There seems to be no occasion for hope. The Lord
was about to hamper Israel's crop, and it was a time of darkness and sorrow.

2. *A Contrast in Harvest Time* (8:3). Each year on the
occasion of the completion of the harvest season there was a
period of rejoicing and celebration. It was a time of feasting
and revelry. Yet, it would not be so when Israel's crop was
gathered. It would be different. Instead of songs of rejoicing
over the harvest there would be wailings; because, instead of
the assurance of continued life suggested by the harvested crop,
Israel's harvest time ("that day") would be one of tragedy and
death. Israel's crop was to be the last crop indeed; they would
be slain. The day of its occurring would result in "the corpses
in multitude, from every place they will be cast forth" — a tragic
parallel to the day of the Lord in 5:18.

On the day of the harvest, after Yahweh had littered Israel
with the dead, they would exclaim, "Silence!" This was not an
exclamation of shock and grief but one suggesting that they
bow before the judgment of their God. They were not to seek
to blame others but simply give up to the tragedy of an opportunity wasted — a privilege misused. The nation had failed God.
What a dismal picture! What a tragic end for God's vineyard!
Israel's fruit, though worthless to God, was the most costly a
nation could produce. It would cost her her life.

3. *The Fruit Israel Bore* (8:4-6). Amos was not alone in
using the theme of fruit and harvest. It was also a favorite
theme of Isaiah as he ministered to the south. In chapter 5
Isaiah called attention to the fact that the fruit borne by "the
house of Israel, and the men of Judah the plant of his delight"

was worthless fruit (Isaiah 5:4b, 7). It was this kind of fruit — worthless fruit — that Amos saw being produced by Israel.

The first fruit to be mentioned was greed (8:4). The wealthy merchants had bought the poor for silver and sold the needy for a pair of shoes (compare 2:6) and sold from an ephah (a standard measure equal to a little more than a bushel — estimated to contain from 1.52 to 2.42 pecks) which had been adjusted, perhaps by use of a false bottom, to hold less than the standard measure. In addition, they were charged with making the shekel great. That is, when they purchased from the poor, they required greater value received than value paid. A shekel in gold has been estimated at $10.80 while one in silver may have been worth as little as 60¢. Whichever may have been referred to here, the crime was the same. Those with the shekel forced those who could not help themselves to give more than just measure for the gold or silver they received in return. Thus, they took every possible advantage of the poor who had brought their produce to the market place in the hope of selling for a reasonable and a livable price.

Israel's greedy merchants added to their guilt by dealing in false balances (8:5b) and selling the refuse (the chaff) in with the wheat (8:6b) as well as grieving over any supposed losses on account of time spent in religious observances (8:5). Israel's fruit was indeed bad and on that account, the vineyard of the Lord would be destroyed (Isaiah 5:6; Amos 8:7 ff.).

4. *The Result of a Crop of Sin* (8:7-14). After having pointed out various examples of Israel's crop, Amos described the inevitable results of having produced such a harvest. God would remember all their works of deceit and injustice (8:7); not one of their cruel deeds would be forgotten; and not one would go unpunished.

A nation with the guilt of Israel deserved the most severe treatment. The judgment, when it came, would take the form of an earthquake or would be as devastating as one. It would result in great upheavals and convulsions in the earth (8:8). These convulsions and upheavals would cause losses of life comparable to that which resulted from the flooding of the river of Egypt. Though, as suggested by some, the comparison does not appear to be a good one because of the lack of suddenness associated with the inundations resulting from the Nile, the emphasis may need to be shifted to the parallel aspect in both flooding and earthquake, which was extent rather than suddenness. If extent rather than suddenness was in the mind of the prophet, then he had chosen well because the destruction which God had in store for Israel was extensive. It would reach from one end of the nation to the other (compare 6:14b).

In addition to destruction on the earth, there would be strange spectacles in the sky. There would be an eclipse which would blot out the sun at noonday (8:9). Such an event had occurred in that part of the world on June 15, 763. It would have been well remembered. The judgment which would fall upon Israel would be comparable to that which came at the time of the eclipse and would result in the same kind of destruction.

After the judgment, the nation would turn to mourning and lamentation. Those surviving the disasters would sit in sackcloth with shaved heads, signs of deepest grief and mourning, and grieve as though an only son (in whom his parents had hope for the future) had been lost in death (8:10). It would be a grief of such staggering proportions that time, the healer of all wounds, would not affect it. The end of the mourning — "its last day" — would be as anguishing as its first day (8:10c). Time would not deaden its pain nor lessen its hurt.

There was still another disaster awaiting Israel. It would exceed all the others. It was a famine marked by a cessation of divine communication with Israel (8:11-14). This famine of the Word of God may have meant that any hope Israel may have had in receiving direction from Yahweh as to how she might be delivered from future judgment was now gone. On the other hand, it could have meant that every word of promise and hope, so often heard in the past, had now been cut off. Either or both of these would leave the nation in graver peril than any of the other expressions of judgment. It would cause even the youth to "faint" from the agonizing and tormenting "thirst" for a word from the Lord (8:13). It was a thirst which could not be slacked by their running from one of their gods to another (8:14). These gods would, in fact, bring a spiritual tragedy which would result in nothing but utter and lasting ruin (8:14c).

Up to this point in his preaching to Israel, Amos had been declaring the truth that sin had its price. That price included natural disasters which destroy their crops, homes, and country-side. It included human disaster coming from war and spiritual disaster resulting from idolatry and the famine of the Word of the Lord. Israel's sin had brought her to the end of the way. "They will fall, and never rise up again" (8:14c). The judgment which they would know was certain because of the nature of their sin and the nature of their God.

5. *The Gatherer of Israel's Crop* (8:2b). The harvester of Israel's crop of sin would be the God who brought her out of Egypt and who had given her the unspeakable privilege and responsibility of being His people. He who had passed by them in mercy while they were in Egypt would now pass through them in judgment. He who had spared them in other days would spare them no more. "The end is come upon my people Israel" (8:2).

The destruction which would engulf Israel was to be the work of the one who controlled the force behind the earthquake and the movement of the planets (8:8, 9). It was the work of one who remembered their unrighteous works (8:7) and demanded repentance and restitution. Their judge was the Lord of conduct (8:4-6) who required justice and righteousness in all human relationships and who called forth His word or caused it to cease at will (8:11). If there had been doubts on the part of Amos's hearers as to God's ability to destroy Israel, Amos had gone a long way toward removing them as he wove the theme of Yahweh's nature and power throughout the message contained in this chapter of his book.

FOR FURTHER STUDY

1. Compare the sins of Amos 8:4-6 with Amos 2:6-8.
2. How great was the potential cost of such evil? Read Amos 8:8-10. What potential resides in the wicked practices of modern society?
3. What ultimate peril is suggested for any wicked nation in 8:11-14? Does this mean a nation is left to its own wisdom? What happens when this is the case? What is the future for a nation without the "words of Jehovah"?

CHAPTER 10

GOD AND THE FUTURE
(Amos 9)

In the mind of Amos there was a vital relationship between God and the future. Israel's future as a nation, based upon what Amos has already said, held little if any hope, but this did not mean that God's purpose in Israel did not have a future. His purpose, though vitally involved with Israel, could not be lost on account of Israel. God's purpose had a future with or without the nation. If the nation failed and it evidently had, Yahweh would realize His purpose through the remnant of Israel. The conditions within Israel, no matter how discouraging, could not alter the purpose which Yahweh had when He chose her and led her out of Egypt. That purpose was the same as Abraham's. It would not fail.

1. *The Discouraging Present* (9:1-4). The final vision of Amos painted a discouraging picture of the present. Rather than seeing symbols of destruction as he had in chapter 8, the prophet envisioned the Lord Himself standing beside the altar (9:1). The first reaction to such a vision would doubtless have been that Yahweh was there to bless, but this was soon abandoned to the realization that He had come to destroy. God's first act was to command that the building (the chief sanctuary at Bethel) be stricken until the pillars toppled and the roof caved in upon the heads of those gathered there (9:1). With a very minor change in the text the phrase which reads "on the head" could be made to read "by an earthquake." If this change were

to be accepted, then the passage would read, "I saw the Lord standing beside the altar: and he said, Smite the capitals, that the thresholds may shake; and break them in pieces by an earthquake all of them; and I will slay . . . ." Since it would be in keeping with the tone of the passage to expect an earthquake as the means of the destruction, this may be the best approach to the passage.

On the other hand, it would still bear the same message if left alone. If by chance some should escape the temple disaster and dig into Sheol (the place of the dead), even there they would not escape the fate decreed by God (9:2a). If he should climb up to heaven, there God would lay hold of him (9:2b). Even those hiding in the numerous caves of Carmel would be sought out and turned over to judgment as well as those who sought to hide at the bottom of the sea (9:3). Not even deportation to a foreign country, which was generally believed to be beyond the reach of Yahweh, would deliver them from the judgment (9:4). Even there they would be slain along with their captors as their captors' enemies would overrun them.

The point the prophet sought to establish was that when Israel fell into the hands of the living God (Hebrews 10:31), there would be no escape. Neither the inaccessible areas (Sheol and heaven), nor the secret recesses of Carmel or the sea, nor the captivity could provide an escape from judgment because God had set His "eyes upon them for evil, and not for good" (9:4).

2. *The God Standing at the Altar* (9:5-10). Many of the group who heard Amos that day were doubtless those who felt that Israel's relationship with God assured her of nothing but favored treatment. They claimed a security and a future superior to that of any peoples of the earth. Such a claim implied that in God's choice of Israel and the subsequent Exodus and covenant they were the only people with whom God had concern and purpose. This being so, they believed that nothing could happen to them because that would suggest failure on God's part, and God could not fail.

Such belief must be met forthrightly. Amos began the rebuttal by pointing to the Ethiopians, the Philistines, and Syrians and declaring that they were where they were because of God's purpose, too (9:7); that is, God had been involved in the circumstances of other men as well as in those in Israel.

Israel was not the only nation for whom there was a purpose in God's plan. His purpose involved others. It was not limited to one nation. He was the omnipotent, omnipresent, omniscient Creator of the *nations* and the universe. He was, therefore, involved in every nation's life, in every activity in the universe. He was the universal God. All nations had a purpose in Him. His relationship to Israel did not eliminate the other nations from His plan for the ages. It simply meant that Israel had been given an opportunity and a privilege to share their faith with them. This was to have been the unique role of Israel even though few ever really saw it.

This God was not to be interpreted as one of the local limited gods of Palestine. Though he stood by the altar, His influence was not confined to it. He had authority over it and wrought mighty works beyond it. He was the One who knew the secrets of Sheol (the abode of the dead) and the hidden places of the sea as well as the hiding places of Carmel and the reaches of heaven (9:2, 3). He was the omniscient God. There were no hidden secrets — no unknown realms with Him.

The God of Israel was also the Creator, mover, and sustainer of the universe. He created the earth and caused it to react to every divine impulse (9:5). The earthquake was the work of His hand. The chambers of heaven were products of His labor, and all creation was made to function at His command (9:6).

Israel's God was also the omnipotent God. He was the all powerful One who could destroy the wicked by whatever means He chose whether by earthquake or famine or marching enemy (9:1 ff.). All the universe was at His disposal to aid in His meting out whatever fate He might determine just and deserving. When He decreed judgment, there would be no escape for the condemned. Their doom was sealed; of this there could be no doubt. One might expect that these words with their message of finality would conclude the message of Amos, as well as God's dealings with Israel, but not so.

In the midst of such a context without any advance warning the prophet declared that this was not all. There was something yet. There was to be a future. God "will not utterly destroy the house of Jacob" (9:8b). The prophet, without negating anything which he had already said, continued and worked beyond it to announce that there would be a future. That future would be filled with glory, and it would be as much the work of God as the past. Yet before the future could be realized Israel must be sifted in the sieve of exile and every faithful servant would be saved from destruction (9:9). All unfaithful would die (9:10). The faithful would form the nucleus or the remnant for the new kingdom of God.

3. *The Glories of the Future* (9:11-15). Despite the destruction of judgment and the disasters of exile, all would not be lost. He who had destroyed could also save. The Lord would save a remnant which would be the basis of the new kingdom of God, to be ruled over by the restored Davidic dynasty.

The time referred to here in the use of "in that day" (9:11) was the time after the judgment had fallen, the unrighteous had been destroyed, and the righteous remnant had been saved. "In that day" God would "raise up the booth of David that is fallen . . . and . . . build it as in the days of old" (9:11). Here the prophet was simply saying that the royal dynasty of David would be raised from its fallen condition to its former glory. God would restore the kingdom and repair the damages sustained by it. Whether this is simply a reference to the destruction resulting from the Exile is questioned by some. It has been suggested that it may have referred to the division of the kingdom in 922 B.C. On the other hand, Amos may have been referring to both the division of the kingdom and the downfall of Israel. He was simply anticipating the time when the nation would attain a glory comparable to that which it enjoyed during David's reign, which would undoubtedly imply the reunion of Israel and Judah as well as the restoration from the destruction of the Exile.

The rebuilding of the Davidic dynasty would provide the nation with strength enough to recapture and rebuild the empire to the limits it knew during David's reign (9:11, 12). Every nation "over which the name of God was called" would be returned to their ancient status of subservience to Israel — the Philistines, the Moabites, the Ammonites, and Syrians. These nations were those which had been conquered by David, yet whose conquest was accredited to Yahweh by him. The words, "over which my name was called," suggest that Yahweh was given credit for the success realized in their capture. They were accredited to the Lord. It was as though the prophet were saying, "As David considered the factors involved in his victories, he recognized God and designated those nations which had been brought into subjection through the Lord's help as 'God's' "; that is, even though David had been involved in their conquest, he declared that as far as the nations were concerned they were really the Lord's and not "Israel's" or "David's" at the point of conquest.

In addition to the rebuilding of the Davidic dynasty the restoration would be characterized by the elimination of famine and want (9:13). The new age would usher in an unparalleled era of fertility. The crops produced "in that day" would be so abundant that it would not be possible to gather them before the plowing and planting seasons came around again (9:13). In fact, the harvest would be so great that it would seem as though the mountains and hills were made of grapes and were giving forth rivers of wine (9:13c). There would be no lack. The day would be one of superabundance. The poverty and need of the past would be no more.

After painting this picture of abundance, Amos reminded his hearers, that those who survive the sifting (9:9) would return to live in such abundance (9:14a). Upon their arrival from Exile, they would rebuild that destroyed by the enemy who had taken them into captivity; that is, they would "build the waste cities and inhabit them" (9:14b). They would plant vineyards and gardens (9:14b).

Beyond returning and planting vineyards and gardens, they

would be able to enjoy the fruits of their labor, something they had not always been able to do before because of the overrunning armies of their enemies. But now they would not be constantly threatened by foreign invaders. They would, on the contrary, exist in a state of security and abundance which would last forever (9:15). They would not again "be plucked up out of their land which" Yahweh "had given them." They would never again be taken from their land nor denied the fruits of their labor.

The hope which Amos had for the future rested in the remnant. The remnant would rebuild the dynasty of David which would exist in abundance and security. These were conditions to be realized in the Messianic Age. Though the prophet did not reach to the personal Messiah, he did describe the conditions which would be established in the Messianic Era. Even so, God was in the process of preparing minds and hearts for the one who would be more fully pictured by those who would come after Amos. Until that time, and it was not to be long (compare Isaiah 9:6 f.; 11:1 ff.), the hope and future glory of the remnant revealed by Amos must suffice.

FOR FURTHER STUDY

1. Read the discussion of "Sheol," pp. 425 ff., in *Theology of the Old Testament* by A. B. Davidson or some other Old Testament Theology.

2. Did Amos come into conflict with any current theological thinking when he suggested that God had a purpose for nations other than Israel? What concept was it? How widespread was it?

3. According to Amos, what was the purpose of the Exile? Have you always seen it as he did in 9:9? What is suggested about God's purpose in the verse?

4. List the aspects of the Messianic Kingdom stated by Amos in 9:11-15. Which of these have been realized? In what way? Discuss.